QUITTING
PLASTIC

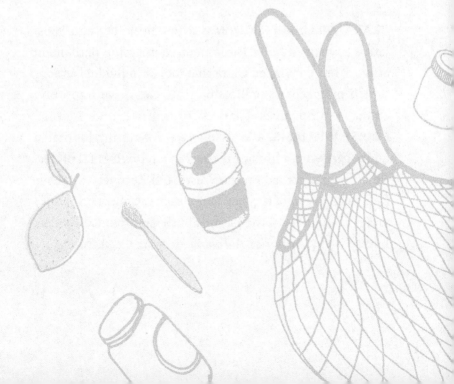

CLARA WILLIAMS ROLDAN is a young policy and legislative advisor in NSW Parliament. Witnessing parliament at work has convinced Clara that lots of individual actions which may seem small at the time can drive important changes in our lives. Clara is writing with her mother, **LOUISE WILLIAMS**, a Walkley-award winning journalist and writer with a lifelong interest in environmental protection. She has served on the Waste and Recovery Strategic Reference Group of the Northern Beaches Council in Sydney and is co-founder of the Baringa Bush Community Garden. Louise is the author of *A True Story of the Great Escape*.

QUITTING
PLASTIC

EASY AND PRACTICAL WAYS TO CUT DOWN THE PLASTIC IN YOUR LIFE

—

CLARA WILLIAMS ROLDAN
WITH LOUISE WILLIAMS

ILLUSTRATIONS BY ELOWYN WILLIAMS ROLDAN

—

ALLEN&UNWIN
SYDNEY · MELBOURNE · AUCKLAND · LONDON

First published in 2019

Allen & Unwin
83 Alexander Street
Crows Nest NSW 2065
Australia
Phone: (61 2) 8425 0100
Email: info@allenandunwin.com
Web: www.allenandunwin.com

A catalogue record for this
book is available from the
National Library of Australia

NATIONAL
LIBRARY
OF AUSTRALIA

ISBN 978 1 76052 871 3

Set in 11/16 pt Stempel Schneidler by Bookhouse, Sydney
Printed and bound in Australia by Griffin Press

10 9 8 7 6 5 4

MIX
Paper from
responsible sources
FSC® C009448

FSC
www.fsc.org

The paper in this book is FSC® certified.
FSC® promotes environmentally responsible,
socially beneficial and economically viable
management of the world's forests.

Dedicated to my wonderful grandmother, Margaret ('Marga'), who passed away during the writing of this book. Thank you for teaching me how to knit, for sharing the books you loved, making the best bolognese ever—and never being 'ordinary'.

We all miss you so much.

CONTENTS

CHAPTER 1

BREAKING UP WITH PLASTIC

I am a 27-year-old eco-warrior. Just kidding. But I do have an issue with plastic and how much we use.

When it comes to reducing plastic, it can sometimes feel like a battle. A battle against the sheer volume of plastic that has crept into virtually every corner of our daily lives. A slog through the immense number of blogs, how-to-guides and #hashtags to find good, practical information about why and how to use less plastic. Sometimes it feels like you've lost before you've even started.

I didn't quit plastic overnight. In fact, I haven't got rid of it entirely. That's partly because plastic is so intrinsic to our lives, quitting will always be a work in progress. And it's also partly because I've discovered there are some plastics we still need. This book is about avoiding the many, many plastics we really can do without.

Everyone has their own reason for wanting to quit plastic. Maybe you want to reduce waste; maybe you just want less stuff filling up your house, your bin and your life. Mine came down to health: my own and that of the environment.

It's no secret that plastic waste is overwhelming our natural environment. What you may not know is that virtually all the plastics ever manufactured are still with us, somewhere on earth. And, of all the plastic wrappers, packaging and bags we use, worldwide, about one-third leak into our oceans and natural environments. While recycling seems like a good solution, the reality is only nine per cent of all the plastics we've manufactured to date has been processed for re-use. Which explains how we have a floating island of plastic in the Pacific Ocean, the great Pacific Garbage Patch, that's almost as big as Queensland. Plastic's durability, which makes it so useful and versatile, also means it doesn't break down like organic materials, leaving it to clog up our waterways and choke our ecosystems, wildlife and sea life. Putting it that way, it seems illogical that such a strong, high-performance material is used to make disposable items that we toss away, often within minutes and without a second thought.

And what about all the plastic we can't see? Microplastics are entering our ecosystems—and the food chain—as plastics break down into tiny fragments. Even washing our clothes is fuelling the problem; synthetic fabrics shed billions of tiny fibres that run off into our waste water.

It's also worth considering that part of what makes plastic so hardwearing are chemical additives such as something called BPA (Bisphenol A). You may recognise it from the number of water bottles, Tupperware containers and even tin cans that now proclaim themselves 'BPA free'. That's because while BPA is great for making plastic more durable, transparent and heat resistant, in the human body it doesn't do such great stuff.

For me, quitting plastic has been an exercise of trial and error. It has been coffee spilled from leaking travel mugs, the absurd Tetris of trying to carry all my groceries in my arms when I've forgotten a reusable bag, and that distinctive odour of sauerkraut that followed me everywhere when I was experimenting with apple cider vinegar as a substitute for hair conditioner. It's also been a family effort, as my first go at the age of sixteen challenged, and eventually galvanised, us all to find creative ways to reduce the plastic in our lives. Which is why I am writing this book with my mum, Louise (who knows a lot about both writing and plastics), why my younger sister, Elowyn, did the illustrations, and why my older sister, Prema—a new mum—was such an invaluable source of information about how to be plastic-free with babies and toddlers.

Over ten years a lot has changed. The clunky online message boards I first sought out have been replaced with communities going 'plastic lite' or 'plastic free' and who are keen to share their tips. They've been followed by innovative businesses and manufacturers offering altern-ative materials—as well as an explosion in research and development (R&D) that is putting more and more plant-based bioplastics and compostable packaging made from plant fibres within reach.

If you are already actively taking steps to reduce your waste, you'll know it's pretty satisfying. I started using a reusable coffee cup in 2010, which, for someone at my level of coffee addiction, adds up to two less disposable cups and lids a day in landfill, for eight years. That's approx-imately 5844 cups (I did the maths). It's powerful to see how much impact you can have as an individual.

LIVING WELL WITH LESS (PLASTIC)

I don't think we realised how much plastic was in our lives until we tried to reduce it.

At first I thought we'd just go cold turkey, but then we realised it would have to be a process.

We wrote lists of things we wanted to change and we researched alternatives and their costs, so it took about three months to transition.

Nowadays we cook a lot more from scratch, make our own nut milks, cleaning products and even face scrubs—but the one thing I haven't solved is where to get corn chips without plastic!

—Aimee Pickles, Christchurch, New Zealand

Aimee, a 26-year-old personal trainer, says there was no single trigger to giving up plastic, just a growing awareness of the damage it was doing, especially as she lives near the coast. So, she and her partner, A.J. Dixson, thought they should 'give quitting plastic a go'. She's found it fascinating and now considers being plastic-free an engaging hobby.

When you decide to quit plastic, it's easy to change your habits if you create consequences for yourself.

If you don't bring a reusable coffee cup, don't have a coffee, or 'drink in'; if you forget your bags, don't go shopping; if you forget a water bottle, use a bubbler or tap. It works!

—Suzie Morris, Caloundra, Queensland

Suzie came face to face with ocean plastics on a holiday in Thailand—and it changed her life. Not only did she see people tossing their rubbish directly into the turquoise waters, snorkelling revealed just as many plastics as fish. When the one-time beautician came home to Sydney, she immediately gave up disposable plastics and shifted industries and states. She moved to Caloundra, where she now runs the local Source Bulk Foods store and hosts workshops about how to live well with less.

I am optimistic, I think there is a new environmental movement coming through.

There is so much awareness out there now about plastics and lots of new small eco businesses are popping up. I know there are lots of people who will still put one orange in a plastic bag—but there are also lots of people passionate about change.

—Shannon Lenihan, Wellington, New Zealand

There was no light-bulb moment for Shannon, a 27-year-old graduate architect, just the long slow realisation that plastic wasn't doing the planet any good. Having been brought up to consider the environment, she started researching plastics as she got older and gradually made the shift. She's learned to make her own beeswax wraps, face scrubs and moisturiser, and doesn't hesitate to email companies and challenge them on plastic packaging. And some do get back to her with new ideas, she says.

Don't underestimate your power as a consumer.

If consumers tell us they would like to buy a certain product but have decided not to because it comes in plastic, we can push that message up the line to the producer.

We've done that recently with a popular product that was in plastic shrink wrap—now it comes 'naked' on an unbleached cardboard backing.

—Joanne Musgrave, Tuggerah, New South Wales, founder Shop Naturally

Struggling with sensitivities to chemicals, Joanne realised she could combine her professional web development skills with her search for the best natural products. After combating her own problems, she decided to establish Shop Naturally, an online sales site linking customers wanting to avoid certain chemicals to innovative eco-businesses. That included reducing the plastics in her life and, more recently, completely eliminating plastic packaging for shipping in her business, right down to swapping plastic packaging tape for water-activated paper tape.

And we've also discovered unexpected benefits. Plastic isn't just a material, it is a lifestyle or even a culture. Plastic has given us drive-through fast-food outlets and anonymous supermarkets groaning with pre-packaged pre-wrapped meals and ingredients from all over the world. Nothing wrong with that. But to reduce our plastic footprint we've had to change the way we shop. We're using smaller local stores that will put our purchases into our own reusable containers or bags, and bulk food shops and farmers' markets. We've also been inspired to try growing our own (it turns out all sorts of things are easy to grow, even on a windowsill). That means we're friendlier with our local communities, we're eating healthier, fresher food, and we're doing more cooking from scratch. It's also pushed us towards decluttering. And, if you think about it, avoiding plastics can also remind us we don't always have to rush. Are we so busy we need to power along the street clutching a take-away coffee cup? Maybe we could follow the Europeans' lead, pause for a moment and enjoy a coffee out of an old-fashioned 'drink in' ceramic cup.

You will, no doubt, find some people who will roll their eyes at your efforts. Why is plastic pollution our problem? Shouldn't governments and businesses be sorting it out? Well, yes, of course. But think about it the other way around. How consumers shop and behave tells businesses and governments a lot, and that drives policies and practices. If we all sat around waiting for someone else to do something, then nothing would happen. Often, it's the small stuff that really matters. Eventually, it does add up to change.

This book is a tool to make reducing the plastics in your life as easy and practical as possible. And it is pretty easy, I promise you. We also look at how the future might pan out. To get you started today, we've broken quitting plastic down into logical steps and room-by-room guides to help you decide what you can quit and what you might use instead. You don't have to do it all. There is no way to fail quitting plastic, because it's a process. Even if you only ditch the big four—the billions of single-use plastic bags, disposable cups, straws and plastic water bottles we use every day—you can make a huge difference.

—*Clara Williams Roldan*

TEN THINGS YOU CAN DO TODAY

1. **Make a resolution** to reduce the plastics you throw away—and post it prominently on social media. Your pride will propel you into action and you'll open up opportunities for conversations with others doing, or thinking about, the same thing.

2. **Buy a metal water bottle and use the tap.** There's no reason for anyone with access to safe, clean water to buy it bottled in plastic. It's not better for us—in fact, tests show almost all bottled water contains microplastics that we ingest.

3. **Stash reusable bags in useful places**—folded in your bag, in the back of the car. (I don't have a car so I use a granny trolley on wheels.)

4. **Carry a reusable coffee cup.** If you forget, don't use a take-away 'just that once', sit down and enjoy your coffee in a real ceramic cup.

5. **Say no to plastic straws and balloons**—convenient and fun for a few minutes or hours, dangerous to wildlife and the environment for decades.

6. **Give up liquid soap and shampoo.** Soap and shampoo bars work just as well and come wrapped in paper.

7. **Swap the cling film** in the kitchen drawer for greaseproof paper or beeswax wraps.

8. **Bake a batch of biscuits**—flour, sugar, butter and eggs are all available in paper or cardboard packaging (and are a great way to reward yourself for your plastic-free efforts).

9. **Eat an ice cream in a cone**—the ultimate waste-free take-away treat!

10. **Pick up a few pieces of plastic litter every day.** Sadly, this is not hard to find. Every bit we take off the street means less plastic washing into the waterways.

CHAPTER 2

GOOD PLASTIC, BAD PLASTIC

Plastic really is fantastic! In about 60 years plastic has transformed life on earth. I don't think there are enough superlatives to adequately describe how much plastic has changed our lives. Virtually anywhere you go on the planet today plastic will be within easy reach, even in Antarctica and at the North Pole. In fact, most of us are wearing it, shod in it, eating and drinking from it, carrying it, sitting on it, walking on it, travelling in it and probably even ingesting it. It's cheap, versatile, convenient, lightweight, strong, waterproof and hygienic—and can even insulate us from electricity.

I can't imagine life pre-plastic. My generation began reaching for plastic as babies, our infant gyms and cots adorned with shiny, colourful, wipe-clean plastic trinkets and toys. You all know how it went from there, whether you were a Lego kid, a Barbie kid, a PlayStation kid or an iPad kid; pretty much everyone except, perhaps, our grand-parents, grew up in Plasticville.

Plastics aren't all bad—or all good—they are an integral part of life on the planet today. So, if you want to cut back on plastics, it is worth knowing what to avoid and why.

Growing up in Plasticville

Humanity's love affair with plastic began in earnest after World War II. Like many technological advances, war sped up the development of a range of plastics that had ini-tially emerged in the early 1900s, or even the late 1800s. It was after World War II that the first of today's workhorse plastics—like Styrofoam, acrylic, nylon and polyethylene—made it out of the lab and into mass, daily use. Life had never looked so bright.

In 1945, Penguin published a book simply called *Plastics*, which anticipated the dawn of a glorious new era. The new plastic man (yes, no gender considerations then) of the future would be born 'into a world of colour and bright shining surfaces where childish hands find nothing to break, no sharp edges, or corners to cut or graze, no crevices to harbour dirt or germs . . . The wall of his nursery, his bath . . . all his toys, his cot, the moulded light perambulator in which he takes the air, the teething ring he bites, the unbreakable bottle he feeds from [are all plastic]. As he grows he cleans his teeth and brushes his hair with plastic brushes, clothes himself in plastic clothes, writes his first lesson with a plastic pen and does his lessons in a book bound with plastic. The windows of his school curtained with plastic cloth entirely grease- and dirt-proof . . . and the frames, like those of his house are of moulded plastic, light and easy to open never requiring any paint.'[1]

How plastic changed the world

So, how exactly did plastic change our world? From the 1940s and '50s mass plastic manufacturing took off and a steady stream of new and 'fabulous' plastics took on traditional materials in virtually every category of production *and* won; replacing paper and glass in packaging, wood in furniture, natural fibres in clothes and carpets, curtains and upholstery and even fluffy toys, rubber in hoses and all sorts of previously 'rubberised' products, and an increasing percentage of the steel and other metals in cars, trucks and aircraft.[2]

It changed the way we live. In a flash, humanity went from the relative scarcity of natural materials and the deprivation of wartime to a utopia of plenty. We had a new, cheap material that appeared to last forever. In 1955 *Time* magazine ran a major feature with the somewhat celebratory title 'Throw Away Living'—it seemed humanity had entered a decadent Golden Age. Cleaning up after ourselves was just another antiquated waste of time, while throwing out more and more disposable items symbolised modernity and efficiency. It represented a triumph over the drudgery of the past. Why wash up if you could just throw the dishes and cutlery away? And plastic was at the forefront of this modern, new world. Sounds great, and in some ways it was—and still is. But if it also sounds too good to be true, that's because it is.

What is plastic anyway?

'Plastic' is just a general term for something that is malleable. At some stage in their production, all plastics flow so they can be moulded, extruded, stretched or cast into any shape, spun into fibres or applied as a coating. It's this versatility that gave plastics their common name.

Most plastics, as we know them today, are made from fossil fuels using the by-products of oil and gas refining. Take, for example, ethylene gas, which would otherwise be discarded by oil refineries. In the 1930s British chemists discovered it could be turned into polyethylene, which makes up much of our packaging, or used to make polypropylene, which is then turned into things like yoghurt tubs, disposable nappies and even car interiors.

What we commonly call plastics are actually synthetic polymers. They start life as basic building blocks called monomers derived from oil and gas, which are linked together into long chains (polymers) and combined with other chemicals. The long chains have a backbone of carbon atoms with hydrogen atoms branching off this spine, as well as a variety of other elements that affect their characteristics, like nitrogen (nylon) and chlorine (PVC). These long chains allow elements to bond in many different combinations and patterns, giving plastics their multitude of properties and enabling chemists and manufacturers to tailor them to almost any purpose.

This might seem like a bit more than most of us need to know, but it is interesting. Why? Because the carbon spine doesn't necessarily have to come from oil and gas. It can come from plants and even bacteria, which are also rich sources of carbon, but, unlike fossil fuels, are renewable and biodegradable.

The first known bioplastic was discovered in 1926 by the French scientist Maurice Lemoigne while he was working with bacteria.[3] However, as oil and gas were cheap and abundant it was of little interest. During the oil crisis of the 1970s, bioplastics were again briefly reconsidered. More recently, there has been intense scientific and commercial interest in making bioplastics using sugar cane, corn and agricultural and forestry waste. These renewable bioplastics are coming onto the market; they're renewable and can be composted after use—and they're coming to supermarkets and take-away food outlets near you! But more about them later.

Good plastic

Before the first plastics were invented (Bakelite, for example, was first produced in 1907[4]—think early retro home phones with numbers and dials), we relied on natural materials that were expensive and relatively difficult to harvest. We used to turn ivory, tortoiseshell, bone, skins, fleeces, rubber, wood, iron, tin, silver, gold, glass, porcelain and even papier-mâché into everyday items, which required lots of effort and put pressure on the natural environment. Elephants, for example, felt this demand keenly. As did all those poor tortoises who provided us with tortoiseshell. The products made from these natural materials were costly, as the finite supply of resources and the hard labour required to harvest them would suggest.

Then along came plastic. Imagine the arrival of a new material that could be fashioned cheaply into almost anything. We were freed from the constraints of the natural world and a whole new treasure trove of products appeared (and they're still coming). Ordinary people could—for the first time in human history—afford lots and lots of colourful, clean stuff. Someone started calling us consumers, and it's stuck.

But cheaper consumer goods were, of course, only one outcome.

Plastics contribute to health and safety by keeping food products fresh for much longer and delaying food spoilage, which, in turn, reduces food waste. Plastic pipes and containers also provide a cheap and effective means for transporting and storing clean water, something fundamental to life. And, as plastics have a very high strength to weight ratio, you don't need a lot of them to do the job. This delivers big energy savings by reducing the weight of packaging, or of consumer products themselves. Plastic packaging, for example, normally makes up only between one and three per cent of the weight of what you buy: 1.5 litres of liquid can be safely stored in a plastic bottle weighing only 38 grams, cheese can be wrapped in 2 grams of plastic film and yoghurt can be stored in a pot weighing less than 5 grams.[5] Comparable glass containers may be up to ten times heavier.[6]

Strong, lightweight plastics have revolutionised transport, too: more can be carried, using much less fuel than in the days of heavy glass and metal packaging. And think about modern vehicles and improvements in fuel economy. Cars are now about fifteen per cent plastic by weight and the Boeing Dreamliner is about 50 per cent plastic by weight.[7] Plastic is also an ideal lightweight and protective casing that helps make products like mobile phones and devices, TVs and computers cheaper and more durable. In construction, plastics are used in lightweight, economic panels, sheets, foams, insulation, pipes, coverings, seals and finishings.

And what about medical devices, which were once made mostly from metal, glass, ceramics and even wood? Over the last 30 years the use of plastics in all kinds of common applications, such as in IV bags, lab equipment, insulin pumps, surgical instruments, catheter bags, face masks, syringes, dental instruments, implants and prosthetics has soared.[8] Plastic is cheap, so it can be disposed of after a single use, greatly reducing the risk of cross infection. Plastic is also smooth and water resistant, and can be manufactured with an antimicrobial additive.[9] Even my grandmother's hip replacement relied on plastic; it set off the alarm going through security at the airport because of its metal parts, but it was the biocompatible plastic lining[10] that allowed her to move smoothly.

Bad plastic

As plastics are so incredibly durable, almost every plastic item we've ever produced is still with us, somewhere on our planet (some have been incinerated). If you are interested enough to be reading this, you've likely seen the footage of a diver making his way through a sea of plastic in Bali, and the distressing and disturbing images of animals that have been killed after ingesting or becoming entangled in plastic. The problem isn't necessarily plastics themselves but the disposable culture that has grown up around them.

We are producing plastics at a blistering pace. Global plastic production increased twenty-fold over the past half century and is forecast to double again in the next twenty years. And much of these are single use. The most obvious example is the plastic shopping bag, still hanging limply at the check-out in many supermarkets and other stores around the world, ready to be filled with groceries that are, themselves, covered in throw-away plastic. An average plastic shopping bag is used for twenty minutes, but it has a 'lifespan' in our environment of hundreds of years. In Australia, five billion plastic bags were handed out at check-outs every year before new bans came into force in some states in 2018—and just four per cent were recycled.[11] In New Zealand it's 1.6 billion[12] plastic bags a year, although a ban announced in 2018 will drive a phase-out. Worldwide, we're using about a trillion—a statistic so big it's almost incomprehensible. What might make more sense is the projection that by 2050 there will be more plastic than fish in the world's oceans, or the discovery of waste plastics in the Mariana Trench, at 11 kilometres below the sea's surface, the world's deepest feature. Of these, 89 per cent were single-use plastics.[13]

Other high-volume single-use plastics are things like straws and disposable coffee cups lined with plastic, and plastic water bottles. Along with plastic bags, these are the big four of waste plastic. They are lightweight, so they 'leak' easily into the environment. They are free, so we don't value them, and they are used only briefly before being tossed. To me, single-use plastic is an obvious place to start; it's easy to bring your own cup, straw, bag or even cutlery. It's also great that in some supermarkets customers are no longer offered free bags and must pay a small charge if they want plastic. A start, but it's not enough.

There are also lots of other short-time-use plastics that end up in the natural environment and begin to break down, finding their way into the stomachs of virtually every species on earth. Think of items like toothbrushes and plastic bottles and lids that are found washed up on distant beaches, and discarded plastic fishing nets that trap countless sea creatures. Half to 80 per cent of all debris found on the world's shorelines is now plastic.[14] In the 1960s, plastics were first found in carcasses of dead seabirds that had mistaken them for food.[15] Since then, 260 species—from invertebrates to sea life and mammals—have been reported ingesting or becoming entangled by plastics. Today, waste plastics contaminate soils and water and have found their way into ecosystems and food chains.

Theoretically, we could be collecting and recycling all this plastic. But we're not. In 2017 scientists worked out how much plastic has ever been produced on earth and where it is now.[16] They found that, as of 2015, humanity had produced 8300 million tonnes of virgin plastics; most of which, 6300 million tonnes or 76 per cent, had already been thrown away. So, where is it all? Only nine per cent has been recycled and twelve per cent has been burned (the equivalent of burning fossil fuels). Most waste plastic remains in the environment, either buried in landfills or as rubbish literally strewn across the planet. The study estimated twice as much plastic waste will have leaked into the environment by 2025. That doesn't mean recycling is futile. Some countries do have good records and many more have announced ambitious targets and plans. But, so far, recycling has fallen (far!) short. This means using less plastic, or quitting plastic, if we want to address the problem at its source.

WHAT ABOUT MICROPLASTICS?

Remember all the panic a couple of years ago about face scrubs and other cosmetics filled with plastic microbeads?[17] We discovered we were dutifully attacking our blackheads and sloughing off our dead skin day and night, then blithely washing plastic microbeads down the drain into our waterways. Now we've got some alternative products available with things like ground apricot kernels and other nice stuff in them. Alas, it turns out, it wasn't just vanity that was plasticising our ecosystems at the micro level.

First, we've got lots and lots of large pieces of plastic slowly breaking down into microplastics in our oceans and freshwater systems and along shorelines and accumulating in soil on land. Beware, for example, of 'degradable' or 'oxo-degradable' plastics often marketed as 'greener' alternatives. All these labels mean is that they break down into lots of tiny pieces of plastic. In Europe, several nations are rolling out bans.[18] Then we've got a whole range of processes and products that deliver very small particles or fibres directly into the environment. One of these is machine washing clothes made from common synthetic fabrics. A synthetic fleece garment sheds about 1.5 grams of tiny plastic fibres per wash.[19] All that active wear, like yoga leggings and gym gear, is also a big culprit because of the fabric it's made from. So, too, are some detergents (pods and tablets) and things like wet wipes made from synthetic fibres, take-away coffee cups (the plastic lining breaks down), and even tennis balls, glitter and teabags.[20]

What happens to microfibres and microplastics is all too quickly becoming apparent; they have been found worldwide. Hundreds of scientific reports have documented microplastics ingested by marine species at every level of the food chain, and from the ocean's surface to the sea floor and from the North to the South Pole.[21] How does this affect us? It's a question of keen scientific interest. We do know that plankton and other small organisms that have ingested microfibres are suffering health issues. We also know that large numbers of fibres have been found in fish and shell-fish sold in markets for human consumption. New Zealand scientists began testing natural and synthetic fabrics and carpet fibres in 2018 to document how different materials break down in water.[22] Cotton and wool fabrics also shed fibres when washed, but initial results suggest that—in contrast to plastics—natural fibres biodegrade fairly quickly.

All of which could seem depressing. But science is about solving problems. The first step is always to identify and understand the challenge. Many people worldwide are working on microplastics and lots of manufacturers are phasing them out or looking for solutions like filters (more about this in Chapter 11, The End of Single-use Plastic?). For us as consumers, knowing more about plastics is a good way we can work out what we want to eliminate and why.

Harmful chemicals in plastics—what to avoid

If the grisly images of marine life maimed and killed by waste plastics aren't enough to get our attention, new Australian research linking plastics to smaller penises probably is. Two University of Melbourne researchers concluded in 2018 that exposure to the chemicals in plastics is 'the number one reproductive issue for men'.

Some of the same chemical additives that make plastics so durable and versatile are in the spotlight, including BPA, found in common packaging plastics called polycarbonates, and phthalates, found in PVC, or polyvinyl chloride, also a familiar household plastic. BPA and phthalates are endocrine disruptors that can mimic the body's natural hormones and have been linked to a long list of health issues such as infertility, obesity, breast cancer, prostate cancer, heart disease and diabetes.[23] A 2014 investigation by *Choice*, one of many worldwide, found food can be contaminated by chemicals from some types of plastic packaging—from fresh meat and cheese to health foods and even organic vegetables.[24]

Choice zoomed in on BPA in many polycarbonates— often used for food storage containers and bottles and to line cans—and phthalates in most PVC (polyvinyl chloride)—used to make cling film and seals for jars and bottles. This is easier to remember if you think of their symbols: number 7 is a polycarbonate; number 3 is a PVC. Both BPA and phthalates have been found in human populations, probably because so many of us experience chronic low-level exposure. The University of Melbourne results are controversial, and regulators worldwide have long claimed low levels of exposure to chemicals via plastics is safe. However, in 2009, a landmark British publication concluded plastics 'present concerns for wildlife and human health' and 'many uncertainties remain'.[25]

There are alternatives: both safer plastics and natural materials. But one thing to take into account is that BPA-free labels don't guarantee a product is safe for use with food or drink. Concerns about BPA are so widespread that many manufacturers are removing it—especially as babies and children are most vulnerable. However, scientists are beginning to question the safety of another substance commonly used to replace BPA—Bisphenol S (BPS). BPS has also recently been found to interfere with the body's hormone system.[26] This is lot to take in, I know. Fortunately, there are many ways to buy food and drink without plastic. One of the easiest switches—and it's much cheaper, too—is to replace bottled water with a stainless-steel bottle filled with tap water.

What plastic is what?

Code	Plastic type	Some uses	Human health risks
1	Polyethylene terephthalate (PET)	• Water and soft-drink bottles • Jars for products such as peanut butter	No known health hazards
2	High density polyethylene (HDPE)	• Milk and cream bottles • Yoghurt containers • Inner bags of cereal packets and similar	No known health hazards

Code	Plastic type	Some uses	Human health risks
3	Polyvinyl chloride (PVC)	• Cling and shrink wrap • Take-away containers • Some soft-drink bottles • Seals on lids or glass jars	Contains plasticisers such as DEHA or phthalates that can leach into food
4	Low density polyethylene (LDPE)	• Take-away containers • Milk carton coating • Bags for bread and frozen food • Cling wrap	No known health hazards
5	Polypropylene (PP)	• Lids for bottles • Yoghurt and margarine containers • Storage boxes	No known health hazards
6	Polystyrene (PS)	• Plastic cutlery • Disposable cups • Coffee cups (PS foam) • Lightweight trays for supermarket packaging	Health risks from traces of styrene monomer investigated and appear to be low
7	All other plastics, including polycarbonate (PC)	• Sauce and condiment bottles • Babies' feeding bottles and infant drinking cups • Reusable water bottles • The lining of food cans	Polycarbonates can release BPA into food, especially when bottles are washed for re-use

Source: Adapted from Choice[27]

CHAPTER 3

OLD HABITS DIE HARD

In just a few generations we've gone from a thrifty ethos of waste not, want not to a disposable culture of waste lots, want more. But we weren't born to 'shop and toss'—we've had to learn how to throw so much away. In the 1950s, after the first coffee vending machines were introduced in offices in the US,[1] workers carefully washed up the plastic cups for re-use. So, too, with the first plastic bags: they could be seen everywhere hanging on our clotheslines. Even in the late 1990s, when disposable coffee cups appeared en masse in Australia and New Zealand, some consumers were initially dubious. Abigail Forsyth, the co-founder of

Melbourne-based KeepCup, remembers the rise of disposable cups in the late 1990s well.

'I had a middle-aged customer tell me he thought it [a disposable cup] made him look like a baby with a "sippy" cup,' she says of her cafe's experience with the transition. 'Now buying a take-away coffee is seen as a signal of "needing" a coffee, you are rushing around doing important things—you don't have time to sit down.'

Disposable coffee cups were just one more convenient addition to our fast-paced lives. Nowadays, we're told we should demand a life *so* convenient that we can slump on our couch after work and summon a beer and hot meal via an app on our phone. We are so busy we need to rush through the supermarket, flinging individually packaged snacks, pre-made meals and plastic-wrapped food into our trolleys. And we are so time-poor we pre-order our 'ready meals' online and have them delivered (festooned in packaging!) to our doorsteps. How do we now unlearn these habits so that we can swim against the current, and, ultimately, help turn the tide?

What about if we begin with the facts? Almost everyone knows about the global plastic scourge. Doesn't that knowledge lead to awareness, then concern, then action? Not necessarily. We are complex, even infuriating, creatures.

Lots of things get in the way of change, including the belief we're not personally responsible for a problem. Then there are practical hurdles, like a lack of time, money or information. Or it might simply be human nature; we are famously better at intending to do something than actually getting around to doing it.

The status quo bias

In reality, old habits die hard. Our fondness for doing today and tomorrow what we did yesterday and the day before that is what psychologists call the 'status quo bias'. We often plod along the same well-worn paths, unless something prods us towards a new fork in the road. We'll often sit in the same seats in class, buy the same make of car and stick with the same health-insurance provider or bank even if the status quo isn't serving us particularly well. Doing the same thing over and over again seems easier, even if there are, in fact, a multitude of other options out there. This common inertia is, in part, about subconsciously choosing the path of least resistance. We're busy, and change requires effort, some kind of personal motivation or prompt. Consumer research tells us that many people keep paying more on mortgages or for their phone or electricity contracts when shopping around could save them money.

There are other forces in play, too. We also like to be part of the herd; our behaviour reflects that of those around us. This powerful herd instinct is used to explain why, for example, we eat sparingly if we go out to dinner with mostly light eaters. Conversely, if we have family members or friends who are overweight, we are at greater risk of being overweight ourselves. Exercise habits are greatly influenced by the herd instinct, too. If our colleagues and friends go to the gym, we are likely to join them.[2] Interestingly, if we walk through an area with lots of litter lying around we are unlikely to pick it up. In fact, we're more likely to litter.[3] This all comes down to the comfort of conformity. We tend to care about what other people think about us and usually overestimate other peoples' interest in our behaviour. This means we can feel silly or hesitant when we go out on a limb. That might be the first time you put a KeepCup on a counter for a barista, if everyone else is using take-away cups. Or when you present your butcher or fishmonger with a reusable container and refuse a plastic bag.

It can be hard to take the first steps. This is especially true if your own contribution to a problem seems remote or miniscule. You probably don't think about the future of our oceans and marine life when you step over a single discarded plastic chip packet. You are just getting through the day. But if you do want to do things differently, psychologists have some encouraging news. Apparently, if you publicly announce your new intention—by telling your friends or family or posting on social media—you will feel some obligation to carry through. You are, for example, more likely to achieve a New Year's resolution you've trumpeted out loud than one you've only said in your head.

What's the trigger for quitting plastic?

We've had hundreds of conversations and done lots of interviews for this book. What we've discovered is that the impetus for quitting plastic is personal. Everyone has a different, unique story. It might be swimming into a swarm of plastic at the beach; or seeing images online of injured, starving or dying marine life; or reading about chemical leaching from plastic; or just realising how ridiculously wasteful it is to devote so many resources and so much energy to making things that are used so briefly before being thrown away.

Change occurs with the right trigger, and sometimes it happens quickly when a critical mass of people finds they're connected by a desire to do something differently. Improvements in the internet make connecting and sharing information and strategies easier than ever. And that's when herds start turning.

There is still, however, a time lag between getting started and confidently saying we've changed the way we do things. There are many, many pop psychology and pseudoscience books and articles purporting to help us break bad habits that propose various time frames for locking in the new you. Real science is far less clear; a major European study[4] concluded that we establish new habits anywhere between eighteen and 254 days! You probably won't notice it, but if you do something new over and over again it sticks. The day will come when you no longer feel comfortable ordering a coffee in a take-away cup or accepting a plastic bag.

THE ULTIMATE INFLUENCER?

I never expected to see the Queen of England (and, yes, I know, Queen of Australia and New Zealand) on the quitting plastic frontline. But I was very pleased when I did.

HRH Queen Elizabeth II did not, of course, use a word like 'quit', but announced with appropriate decorum, through her Buckingham Palace spokesperson, that there was a 'strong desire to tackle the [waste plastic] issue' in the royal household.

Apparently inspired by the globally renowned British naturalist and conservationist David Attenborough—who has been known to stroll through the palace gardens with the Queen—the palace announced in early 2018 the phasing out of plastic straws in the public cafes of its various properties and a ban in staff cafes. Internal caterers at Buckingham Palace, Windsor Castle and Holyrood Palace would only be permitted to use china plates and glasses, or recyclable paper cups.[5]

The royal rejection of disposable plastics came in time for the wedding of Meghan Markle and Prince Harry,[6] who, in lieu of gifts, provided guests with a list of charities they might like to donate to, including one tackling marine plastic pollution. Princess Eugenie upped the ante by announcing her October 2018 wedding to Jack Brooksbank—and their marital home—would be plastic-free.[7]

Does the royal family's stance on plastic matter? Although it's not making the cover of the tabloid mags, I think it does.

The Anglican Church (of which the Queen is Supreme Governor) has since used its church network to appeal to followers to quit plastic for Lent. Churches provided practical tips and advice and the Lent plastic-fast inspired scores of media columns and blogs.

Theresa May, the UK prime minister, then announced plans to ban the sale of various single-use plastics, including plastic straws and cotton swabs. A consortium of 40 major business followed with a pledge to eradicate single-use plastic packaging. This includes major food and non-food brands—such as Sainsbury's, Nestlé and Coca-Cola—that are collectively responsible for more than 80 per cent of the UK's supermarket plastic packaging.

There has been plenty of criticism of these aspirational plans as too weak. Action, too, seems far off in the future. But the plastics issue is on the public and political agenda. And as far as figureheads go, the Queen is definitely not too shabby.

A creative approach to driving change

When KeepCup was launched back in 2009, its goal was to reduce cafe waste by initiating behavioural change. The cup was designed to replicate a take-away cup, so it would fit seamlessly into the existing service flow, just without the rubbish. It was an interesting product because it was specifically designed to make change easy, just as disposable coffee cups seemed easy a couple of decades ago. It had to be easy to unlearn old habits and replace them with new.

Even so, it was dismissed by one designer at the time as 'the stupidest idea ever'.[8] KeepCup is now operating in 65 countries and estimates the five million or so cups it's sold globally have prevented ten billion or so disposable cups going into landfill. Many copycat products, too, are emerging on the market.[9]

'We had to work with cafes so that customers would feel it was okay to bring in reusable cups. People don't like making a fuss, they were worried they would interrupt the barista, or were embarrassed,' Ms Forsyth says.

What has driven that turnaround in some sections of our cafe culture? KeepCup originally targeted the people who could influence others by signalling it was okay to reuse a cup.

'If people see someone they respect with a reusable cup, that influences their behaviour. Primarily this was baristas and independent cafes, but equally if the boss is carrying a reusable cup around it sets the tone,' she says.

Sociology and behavioural psychology back this up. We are, indeed, more likely to behave in a particular way if we think someone important to us expects this behaviour. Marketers also know that if we believe most people are doing something, we are gripped by FOMO and want to be included.

I am not entirely sure how to make quitting plastic cool, but if you are going to do it, a bit of swagger won't hurt. I am optimistic that reducing plastic is catching on— just look at the uptake of reusable coffee cups and metal water bottles, for example. This might seem naive, but I am happy to keep chipping away. And, when lots of people start to behave differently, then the herd instinct becomes very useful, sweeping up lots of people along the way.

CHAPTER 4

GETTING STARTED

Just do it? Well, sort of.

If you want to succeed, you need to think about how it's going to work for you, personally. Currently, the path of least resistance is, certainly, the one that runs alongside all those groaning supermarket shelves packed with a dazzling array of convenient, functional and familiar plastic-wrapped goods. Forging a new path may seem like a challenging and lonely slog. This sounds a bit melodramatic but it's not. Often the most difficult things to change are those we do every day. It's much easier if you are in a warm fuzzy crowd of peers swapping tips than if you are heading off in a new direction on your own. So, step one might even be to find a like-minded friend.

Think about your own character

Are you an all-or-nothing type? Is plasticised convenience an addiction you need to quit cold turkey? Or are you the type of person who can gradually cut down, one plastic bag or bottle at a time? Could you pick one item, or a couple of items, and start with them, or even one room in the house? What happens when it all gets too hard? Are you someone who just gives up? I'm thinking eating ice cream straight out of the tub or a whole block of chocolate here. In my family there are multiple personality types, so we know failure at pretty much every level. Which has also taught us how to regroup and start again.

Think about making an impact

The most common single-use plastics found in the environment worldwide are, in order of scale, cigarette butts, drinking bottles and caps, food wrappers, grocery bags, lids, straws and stirrers, other thicker bags, and polystyrene foam take-away containers.[1] Maybe start by picking from this list.

What about the cost?

Isn't plastic-free more expensive? Sometimes it can be. If you swap synthetic clothes for wool, cotton or bamboo, you'll probably pay more if you compare single item costs, but not necessarily if you compare quality. And if you swap disposable nappies for fitted cloth nappies you'll pay a lot less. But price is a valid issue, which is why we've considered costs for every category we've looked at.

Amy Kirk, store manager at the plastic-free family business Scoop Wholefoods, suggests backing up practical action by rethinking our attitudes to shopping.

'With huge supermarkets we seem to have developed a siege mentality—as though we have to stock up on absolutely everything when what we really need to do is to buy just as much as we need at the time.'

At Scoop's six stores across New South Wales, ingredients are sold by weight into paper bags or your own containers. Amy says customers often come into the store with their own recipes and buy only what they need, instead of buying big plastic packets that end up at the back of the pantry until they are stale or out of date and then must be thrown out. This saves money, even if some ingredients are more expensive by weight than jumbo supermarket specials. This, she says, is a very practical solution to the 'War on Waste', totally eliminating single-use plastics.

'Sometimes people apologise for spending so little—they might only buy 25 cents' worth of something like cinnamon or a dried herb. But I really like it—you never need to apologise for buying just enough that you won't end up with any waste!'

Does what I do really matter?

Angus Harris 'believes 100 per cent' in the power of consumers. As the co-CEO of Harris Farm Markets—which removed all single-use plastic bags from the check-outs of their 26 Australian stores at the beginning of 2018—he's been watching the plastic debate closely.

'People pushed us over time to address single-use plastic bags—we weren't at the forefront of the movement, we were responding to feedback,' he says. Notwithstanding, the company's decision to remove plastic bags ahead of other large competitors had an immediate impact.

'We went from 24–25 million plastic bags a year down to zero overnight—and we were humbled by the overwhelming positive response of our customers for the #BanTheBag movement.'

Harris Farm initially offered free paper bags to customers, then shifted to passing on the cost of 20 cents per bag. It quickly went from 2.5 plastic bags per customer to 0.7 paper bags, then down to 0.4, as shoppers brought their own bags or took cardboard boxes.

Right across the business, Angus has been working out ways to remove more plastics, like introducing a filtered water station for bottles to be refilled at one store, to making some stock—like pulses, beans, nuts, dried fruit and snacks—available to scoop directly into paper bags, and using plant-based bioplastic containers and glass jars.

'Although I know convenience will win every time with some customers, I am cautiously optimistic,' he says of the changes coming through.

Strategies for getting started

The good news is that you've already taken the first steps. Many of the people we spoke to said just starting to think about plastic was the key to seeing opportunities to use less. It's also useful to turn to some tried and true strategies. We don't need to reinvent the wheel.

You might recall the sage advice of the US activist and commentator Michael Pollan, who advised that the key to healthy eating was simple: 'Eat food. Not too much. Mostly plants.'[2] To which he added, 'Don't eat anything your great-grandmother wouldn't recognize as food.' In one fell swoop, Pollan eliminates all those overpackaged, overprocessed, additive- and preservative-laden foods that are simultaneously ruining our health and expanding our waistlines. Just the kind of foods that currently come swathed in plastic.

So, if you're thinking about quitting plastic, you'll find you'll also be quitting lots of processed snack foods that are only available in plastic. Instead, you'll be buying a lot more 'wholefood' ingredients and, like your grandmother and great-grandmother, you'll have a chance to enjoy the taste and health benefits of cooking from scratch.

When it comes to plastic-free shopping, your grand-mother's life experience is just as useful. Think of your grandparents, or other older members of the community, as invaluable fountains of information; they've shopped pre-plastic and lived to tell the tale. They're the time travellers who live among us and, like the trope of the fictional time travellers, they are here to help us navigate the future. Just as long as we take the time to ask them how they did it. You'll come up with a long list of great ideas to help you waste not and want not, like keeping a cardboard box in

AN ACCIDENTAL (ANTI-PLASTIC) ACTIVIST

When Natalie Warren arrived in Sydney from grimy central London in 2011, she was initially stunned by the beauty of the city's beaches and the joy of commuting to work by ferry. But, as the months wore on, she began to notice something less appealing, especially on the northern beaches where she and her husband had settled.

Everywhere she looked, says the 37-year-old actuary, there was rubbish.

'In London everything is so grey and grubby, you don't notice as much—but seeing plastic waste, coffee cups, take-away containers and straws lying around in such a naturally beautiful environment is so incongruous. I realised things weren't perfect.'

Her first reaction was to try to do something to help. She joined 'Responsible Runners' and spent endless weekends running with rubbish bags up and down Manly Beach, but the litter—and the plastic washing up along the tideline—was always back the next day. Sometimes, Nat and her group saw people eating on the sand, then just walking away without even bothering to take their rubbish to the bins.

'At times it was exhausting, even soul destroying. I realised it was useless to just clean up after other people if you didn't try to do something about reducing plastic pollution at the source.'

In her own life, she'd cut out lots of plastics, especially the big four—single-use plastic bags, water bottles, straws and take-away coffee cups. Then she took another more unusual step.

Nat stood for election on the large council that manages Sydney's northern beaches region of some 250,000 people—and was elected on an environmental ticket.

Then she joined forces with other volunteers who, like her, devoted lots of their energy and time to removing plastics from the marine environment, especially plastic straws. She realised the council could do something with long-term impact. Her first motion as a councillor was carried—formalising council support for the phasing out of plastic straws in a region of scores of beaches, and a ban on the use of plastic straws in new leases for council properties, including surf clubs.

'You have to believe in your individual impact,' she says.

'You can be someone who makes other people feel differently about an issue, and if they see you doing something like reducing plastic they might think "that's something I should be doing too".'

Now with a young baby, Nat and her family are still keen to reduce their own plastic footprint.

But, she says, 'I'm not a saint, it's not always possible to avoid plastic entirely. I just do all the things that are easy—if everyone did them it would make a huge difference.'

the back of the car, investing in a shopping trolley, or jeep, or some string bags or asking the butcher to go back to butchers' paper. They shopped locally and seasonally, so they didn't waste a thing. They planned meals ahead and cooked from scratch—and pickled and preserved surplus. The curse of the overabundance of today is waste. Our grandparents valued food because they knew what it was to have too little. We should be a generation who understand the risks of having too much.

The environmental three 'Rs' of waste management are also useful—*Reduce* what you consume, then *Re-use* rather than throw away, and only then *Recycle*. We've thrown a couple more Rs in.

✔ REFUSE

This is simple. Just say no to plastic bags, bottled water and all those easy things to avoid.

✔ REDUCE

Can't we just buy less stuff?

Today, we humans consume eight times more resources worldwide than a century ago. And while we used to consume mostly renewable biomass, like wood and other plant materials such as cotton, we've shifted to mostly fossil fuels—that are used to make plastics and synthetic fabrics—and minerals and ores.[3] We're on track to double the amount of plastic we use over the next twenty years.[4] And in just ten years, we've doubled how much we throw away, to 1.2 kilograms per person per day in our cities.[5] Can't we just buy less plastic stuff and avoid plastic packaging?

✔ REPLACE

Look for alternatives to plastic goods and packaging.

There are lots of swaps out there that make reducing plastic easy, like swapping plastic-wrapped for 'naked' or paper-wrapped food or goods. What about buying a ceramic or china butter dish and using paper-wrapped butter instead of a plastic tub of spreadable? What about using a wooden spoon instead of a plastic one? And keep an eye out for compostable bioplastics made from renewable feedstocks like agricultural waste. There are lots of opportunities to replace plastics with something kinder to the environment.

✔ RE-USE

What can we do with all that stuff we already have?

Look around your home. Can you re-use all those old containers by finding stores that are willing to **refill** them? More and more shops are encouraging you to bring in your own containers—and may even reduce the price if you do. And what about using clothes for longer than the fashion cycle might dictate? It might not seem obvious but most of us dress in synthetic fabrics—which are plastics—and so are just as problematic as much of the packaging we throw away. You don't have to buy new for variety, you can swap clothes with friends.

 **RECYCLE**

Not a magic bullet, but a part of the solution.

China's decision to stop importing waste from other nations in 2018 has left growing stockpiles of waste across Australia and New Zealand and elsewhere. Of the main waste categories—paper, plastics, glass and metals—plastics are the most problematic. In 2016–17, Australia recycled a total of just 11.8 per cent of its plastic waste (more than half of which was previously sent to China[6]). New Zealand doesn't publish national recycling statistics, but media reports point to similarly low plastic recycling rates.[7] In the long term, pressure from consumers—and pledges by big businesses to increase recycling—should bolster local recycling. In the meantime, the only real solution to plastic pollution is using less.

CHAPTER 5

THE KITCHEN

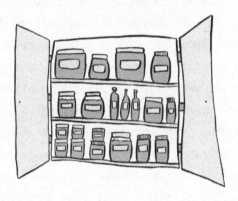

Food glorious food, (almost) all wrapped in plastic! We live in a world in which plastic wrapping and fresh food have become virtually synonymous. So, what do we do without its fabulous properties that enable us to extend the shelf life and maintain the freshness of all sorts of things, from meat to snacks and ready-meals?

When it comes to the kitchen, start with what's easy. Then build up to the more complicated challenges. You'd be surprised at how much plastic you can avoid with a few simple changes.

Easy kitchen solutions

Sometimes when I am slogging away at the gym, my mind wanders. I imagine what aliens looking down on us would make of my inexpert attempts at bizarrely named exercises like 'burpees', 'kettle-bell swings' or 'hammer woodchops'. The same goes for how we shop. What on earth (aliens, ha ha) are we doing sorting each type of fruit and veg into a separate plastic bag or picking them up on trays covered in cling wrap—when we are only going to dump them, wantonly intermingled, into fruit bowls and crispers? Bagging and packaging can make the check-out process easier, especially now that we're often serving ourselves. But what about bunches of bananas, single avocados or truss tomatoes, all naturally designed (skin and stems) for easy handling?

There's a simple solution—don't pull off handfuls of flimsy plastic fruit and veg bags every shop. Let your fruit and veggies go naked in the trolley. Alternatively, it's easy to bring your own reusable net or mesh bags (look online, or in some stores) for those purchases too difficult to juggle (think brussels sprouts, salad leaves, peas). In one fell swoop you could avoid hundreds or even thousands of plastic bags a year, with no impact on the convenience of your shop or the quality of your purchases. In 2016–17 Australians used 5.66 billion single-use plastic bags, for an average of about twenty minutes each, before throwing them out. Which does make you wonder—how did people manage pre-plastics? This might just offer us a few tips.

What history can tell us

The first recorded use of packaging for food was in 1035; a Persian traveller visiting markets in Cairo saw that vegetables and spices were sold to customers wrapped in **paper**.[1] This rather ordinary observation must have seemed very interesting at the time. We didn't need food packaging when food was grown and sourced locally and either traded within communities or sold at local markets, and put straight into baskets or wrapped in leaves.

Early travellers too, those pioneers of globalisation, could mostly get by on local food. Not so, however, when they were separated from food sources over any extended period of time or found themselves in hostile territory far from home. Think of all those lengthy voyages on sailing ships—and of those poor Galápagos tortoises boarded alive to be used at sea for the potable fluid held in their 'neck bags' and their meat. Like so many other technological innovations, humankind's long history of warfare also ushered in various new ways to survive, including keeping ourselves fed. At the end of the eighteenth century, Napoleon Bonaparte's French government famously admitted they were losing more troops to hunger and scurvy than to battlefield clashes. So, in 1795, they offered a fantastic reward to anyone who could invent a method of preserving food for the French army and navy. Nicolas Appert, a former candy maker, brewer and pickle maker, came up with a solution in 1809. Appert successfully preserved food by partially cooking it, sealing it in bottles with cork stoppers and placing the containers in boiling water.[2] His first 'partridges, vegetables and gravy' meals in **glass containers** were used successfully to feed Napoleon's navy for four months, and his preservation method paved the way for the development of a more robust food container, the **tin can**.

We didn't even think about **individual packaging** until the end of the nineteenth century. Like all generic products of the time, biscuits came in large barrels and were scooped out by grocers and sold by weight. But in 1890 when the US National Biscuit Company developed a lighter, flakier biscuit they realised their product needed more protection—so they introduced a paper package with an inner liner that would preserve it. With it came a new opportunity to 'brand' goods using their wrapping, to distinguish them in the marketplace.

The arrival of plastics

World War II rapidly accelerated the development of plastics, and so ushered in their mass peace-time application from the late 1940s. Polyethylene food wrap (better known by its trade name Saran wrap or cling wrap), for example, was initially sprayed on US fighter planes to protect them from the elements. In 1949 it went on the market as the clingy, plastic wrap we know today. Plastic packaging and food seemed like they were made for each other—especially as refrigerators simultaneously became standard household items. And as supermarkets replaced open markets, corner stores and small grocers, packaging became increasingly important commercially. With no friendly grocer to help us choose our products, it was packaging that attracted browsing buyers—and shouted out to entice them—as they made their way along anonymous supermarket aisles.

I am hoping this somewhat breathless race through how we got to where we are today reveals more than my googling skills. Can history help us with the contemporary challenge of decoupling shopping from plastic packaging? How might we now get on with our (busy) lives with less plastic? Can we go back to using farmers' markets and smaller shops, where we engage personally with sales people who offer us alternatives like paper bags? Should we go back to some of those earlier packaging options— paper, glass jars and metal cans? Can we better plan meals so we buy less and shop more often—to avoid wasting food and using plastic packaging? (Over-purchasing and poor planning mean Australians waste $20 billion worth of food a year.) Or can we pressure supermarkets, other retailers and food processors to solve the problem for us with new compostable bioplastics made from plants and other renewables?

Yes, to all of the above. Do these options also demand some level of compromise on your part? Yes, again.

Reducing the plastics in your kitchen will likely turn out to be your own personal mix of old practices, new discoveries and compromises. The unexpected pleasures and benefits of filling the pantry and fridge without bringing home mountains of plastic packaging are, in my opinion, part of the fun.

Filling the pantry and fridge—a food packaging hierarchy

Go naked—Bring your own bags, jars, containers and string bags for fruit, veggies, meat, fish and other staples and snacks. Accepting no disposable packaging wins every time—no resources or energy are wasted, plus you know exactly what you are buying and how fresh it really is.

Metal packaging—Choosing **metal cans, tubes or containers** over plastic has some benefits—and some potential drawbacks. Metals are both valuable and perfectly recyclable; their properties don't degrade with reprocessing. In Australia, 88 per cent of metal waste is recovered for recycling or re-use—the highest recovery rate of any material.[3] And almost all aluminium is recovered. Other countries have similarly high metal recycling rates. But metal packaging can be heavy, so more energy is needed for transport. And metal recycling is a high-energy, high-temperature process. Cans are also usually lined with a thin film of plastic, which may contain BPA, a known health risk. However, Food Standards Australia and New Zealand says[4] the latest scientific evidence suggests concentrations of BPA in can linings are too low to impact our health.

Glass jars and bottles—These are great for preserving and storing food. But they are heavy to transport and are fragile. The many different types of glass can make recycling challenging and waste glass stockpiles are building up worldwide. Look for suppliers who will refill a glass jar—instead of buying a new one every time—and re-use jars at home.

Paper and cardboard packaging—This is renewable and easy to recycle or compost. But big increases in demand for paper products could drive further land clearing for forestry plantations.

Compostable plant-based bioplastics—Bioplastics are a rapidly growing sector (see Chapter 11, The End of Single-use Plastic?) but challenges remain, including consumer confusion and the need for industrial composters to ensure they break down. If bioplastics end up in landfill, they generate emissions like other waste.

Recycled plastic—Much better than virgin plastic, but read labels carefully. It is very easy to be confused by a friendly looking 'Recyclable' symbol, which just means the packaging *could* be recycled, not that it will be recycled.

Degradable and biodegradable plastics—These labels can be misleading. Degradable or oxo-degradable just means the plastic will break up into very small pieces of plastic. Biodegradable means it will break down, probably as bacteria consume it—but this may take years.

Where can I shop plastic-free?

Bulk stores

These are popping up everywhere under the banner of plastic-free or waste-free shopping. They're an interesting hybrid of old and new. On the one hand, they hark back to the traditional grocer who scooped basic dry foodstuffs— like flour, sugar, rice, oats—out of large bins into paper bags or paper wrapping. But today's versions are self-serve and there's a lot more on offer than the old-time staples: from muesli and breakfast cereals to chocolates, snack foods and ground nut butters, as well as loads of varieties of rice, pasta, grains, sugars and flour. It's a good way to cut out plastic packaging altogether. Bulk produce is sold from clear closed bins with hinged lids marked with the country of origin and other product details. You can bring in your own jars or containers and (after they are weighed) scoop produce directly into them. Or you can use the paper bags provided. Some bulk stores also refill bottles with cleaning products and personal care products, like shampoo and conditioner.

Both Australia and New Zealand have online bulk stores that ship goods to you in brown paper boxes and bags.

Verdict   With some careful planning you can fill a couple of shopping bags with jars of your weekly staples and snacks without any packaging at all, or with just a handful of compostable or recyclable brown paper bags. You can also buy exactly what you need, avoiding the waste that is inevitable when you go for jumbo packs on special at the supermarket.

The potential downside is less choice—and even, perhaps, an uneasy feeling as you move away from the familiarity of trusted brands. Shopping also can take longer (although the shops are small and unpacking directly into the pantry is fast and satisfying). A lot of products are more expensive than supermarkets by weight. But I love bulk stores because I waste virtually nothing and I eat better because I'm cooking more of my food from scratch. To find your nearest bulk store anywhere in the world, go to www. zerowastehome.com and click on Bulk Finder.

SEARCH TERMS   Q bulk food stores   Q bulk wholefoods   Q wholefoods in bulk bins.

PLASTIC-FREE SHOPPING—COMING TO A MALL NEAR YOU

Just over a decade ago Paul Medeiros and his wife, Emma Smith, fled high-pressure city jobs to start a new life in the country. Today, they are leading an international rollout of a disruptive retail model that enables consumers to shop entirely without plastic—all from their rural base. In the process, they've avoided the use of some 50 million plastic bags.

Paul and Emma are the founders of The Source Bulk Foods, which is currently adding a new store every six weeks to its 43 stores across Australia, New Zealand and the United Kingdom.

The retail model goes back to the couple's first foray into food retailing in 2007 when they left inner-city Sydney for Mullumbimby in the green hinterland of northern New South Wales, a region long favoured by sustainability-minded communities.

Unsurprisingly, Mullumbimby locals embraced the opportunity to buy hundreds of products without packaging, by scooping them from bulk bins into their own containers or paper bags and paying by weight. And, as Paul and Emma also wanted to offer healthier alternatives to processed supermarket products, northern

New South Wales was just the right demographic for their largely natural and organic range.

When the couple trialled the model in the city, initially in Sydney, it also worked.

'We both previously worked in city jobs for big retailers—in my case for a company that was putting small local shops out of business. We had an epiphany, we'd come to a fork in the road,' says Paul of their decision to leave the city behind.

'We gave up well-paid jobs, we simplified our lives. We bought a fruit shop in Mullumbimby, which we gradually transformed into the first Source Bulk Foods store,' he says.

Bulk food stores, themselves, are not new; in the pre-supermarket era, grocers scooped bulk goods into brown paper bags and sold them by weight, and some local food co-ops and health-food stores maintained that tradition.

The rapid expansion of The Source and similar bulk food stores into modern retail districts reveals a pent-up demand for an alternative to grab-and-go packaged food.

A new generation of bulk stores is, says Paul, 'drawing people out of the woodwork'. They are consumers interested in waste reduction and sustainability who have long been starved of choices in the way they shop.

'After decades of supermarket dominance, a growing plastic-free, waste-free consumer market is now pushing back. The supermarkets are paying attention. Bulk stores are no longer just a niche market and waste is no longer a niche concern,' he says of the growing awareness of plastic pollution.

It is unsurprising, then, that an increasing number of supermarkets and other food retailers are offering a small number of their products unpackaged, and from bulk bins. A recent industry report found that the environmental consumer, once largely overlooked as a vocal minority, is more influential than retailers had long thought. Fifty percent of Australians believe food and drinks products are overpackaged and 69 per cent say they would consider boycotting a product that didn't meet their environmental criteria.[5]

That said, Paul concedes that removing plastic at the point of sale is the easiest part. Working out how much plastic is in the grocery supply chain and what to do about it is much trickier. Virtually every pallet transported any distance is wrapped in cling film, and many bulk foods arrive at the store in large plastic containers or plastic-lined boxes.

That's the next challenge, he says. One solution is working with suppliers to replace plastic linings with bioplastics made from corn—but it's still a work in progress.

Local and farmers' markets

Yay! Markets are back pretty much everywhere. If you haven't already stumbled across local bakers, cooks and producers setting up their wares, search online for a market near you. Most suburbs and towns have markets at least once a week where you can buy a cardboard box of fruit and veg and lots of other fare without packaging. One near us has great take-away food—and no disposable containers. Instead, there is a crockery and cutlery booth that lends you a plate or bowl and spoon and fork, which are then washed up on their return. Given that our charity shops are overflowing with good-quality china, crockery and cutlery, it's a great way to give it another outing.

On the north island of New Zealand in Whangarei there's an innovative food co-op that brings online shopping and local food production together. The region is packed with small-scale producers and hobby farmers who offer their crops and farm products like eggs and honey on the co-op website. You can browse and shop online in much the same way as you would on a supermarket website, but choice depends on what's in season. The co-op boxes up orders for local collection or delivery. This is about the easiest way I know to buy seasonal, local, fresh produce. So, look for co-ops near you.

If you can, grow your own; there's no packaging involved. (Get any soil, soil conditioners or mulch delivered in bulk, rather than buying them in plastic bags.) Anyone can grow something. I now live in a tiny inner-city apartment with no balcony, but I grow herbs on the windowsills, which is much cheaper than buying them and means I don't have herbs wilting in the fridge. You can also try crop swap—there are groups everywhere—as a free way to swap the excess from your own garden for something different, while making new social connections.

Verdict Loads of enjoyable plastic-free and personalised shopping options are available at markets everywhere. Prices are often higher by weight than supermarkets but keep the budget under control by buying only exactly what you need.

SEARCH TERMS 🔍 Australian Farmers' Markets 🔍 local markets food co-ops 🔍 local harvest 🔍 crop swap 🔍 food swap.

Butchers, fishmongers, greengrocers, bakeries, delis etc.

I could fill the rest of the book with stories about being the first person to offer a container over the counter at the butcher or the fishmonger. But I think the gold medal for awkward experiences goes to my mum. She took a container into a major supermarket and handed it in at the butchery section and asked for some chicken wings (she would like me to clarify here that they weren't for her, as she has been a vegetarian for 40 years—they were for the cat). The young guy was so confused he asked her if she was planning to shoplift. After some discussion he conceded the wings were so cheap they weren't worth stealing, but he remained unconvinced by this change in routine. The next hurdle was the self-serve check-out; the weight of the container froze the machine and drew the attention of the assistant.

Many others have experienced the disappointment of their purchases being put into a plastic bag first to be weighed, then that brand-new bag (only in use for a few seconds) blithely chucked into the bin. So, you may have to work on your spiel: mention that you're avoiding plastic, then explain that scales can be zeroed to avoid adding the weight of the container to your bill, and smile!

You may also find a business that refuses your container outright on 'hygiene grounds'. This is a bit of a grey area as the Food Standards Australia and New Zealand (FSANZ) code requires only that a container 'is fit for its intended use' and is unlikely to cause contamination before or during the packaging process. Which really means that bringing your own clean, dry container doesn't breach any food safety standards. However, stores that don't like the perceived hassle can, of course, just say no to your business.[6]

Do persist, as lots of small stores are happy to oblige and, if you do strike up a conversation, shopping become much more personal. As well as butchers and fishmongers, local providores can help. They often offer cheese cut from a waxed wheel that can be wrapped in paper. Ditto lots of salads, charcuterie, dips, soups and meals that can be spooned directly into your own containers. By weight, they are more expensive than supermarkets, but allow you to buy only what you need.

For bread, shop at your local bakery. Most bakers are happy to put your loaf, sliced or not, into a paper bag. Otherwise, bring a reusable bread bag that keeps bread fresher for longer, and can also go into the fridge or freezer.

Verdict Don't give up too easily on bringing your own containers! It gets easier and you can establish good relationships with your local stores once they get to know you. Many will support what you are doing. If they don't, there are plenty of other places to shop.

SEARCH TERMS Q your local butchers Q bakers Q fishmongers and providores Q food containers Q food storage Q reusable food containers.

FAST FOOD WITHOUT THE PLASTIC

Contrary to popular belief, it *is* possible to pick up a healthy ready meal without the plastic packaging.

At The Butcher and the Chef in Sydney's north, family dishes like meatloaf, stuffed chicken and homemade chicken nuggets are ready to go in compostable oven-proof trays that can go straight into the oven. If you want to cook a steak, they also offer scalloped potatoes and red wine jus on the side, similarly plastic-free.

'It is all about trying to find those easy solutions for customers to grab and go,' says co-owner Kristy Barbara of their range. At the same time, however, she and her husband Tom are committed to running a plastic-free food business. Since they made the switch about three years ago they've avoided handing out almost a million single-use plastic bags and tens of thousands of plastic sheets, previously used for ham and other sliced smallgoods. Instead, they wrap their meat in recycled brown paper and use returnable glass jars for their other products like pesto, bone broths, tapenade, lima beans, nuts and sweet biscuits. Even the gloves they use for food handling are natural latex (rubber), not plastic.

'I have been in the meat industry for 25 years. As a business owner with three young children, I want to take what I do at home and bring it into the business. That means helping my customers and my community introduce more plastic-free products into their life,' she says.

At first, The Butcher and the Chef only removed the plastic sheets used for smallgoods and started up conversations with customers about paper versus plastic. The overwhelming majority of customers said they preferred paper wrapping. That was enough encouragement to announce all plastic was out.

However, quitting plastic comes at a cost. Instead of a plastic bag for 1 cent, the business is using recycled baking paper from Norway at 17 cents a sheet, as no suitable paper wrapping is yet available in Australia. In the competitive retail meat business, meat prices can't be hiked to match, so other high-value products, like homemade pesto, currently cross-subsidise the paper packaging.

Ultimately, Kristy's goal is to do away with single-use packaging altogether. In the long term, importing paper is not sustainable, she says. The business offers customers a ten per cent discount if they bring in their own container that can go into a reusable shopping bag, then straight into the fridge. Likewise, the jars used for packaging sauces and accompaniments can be returned for a small refund.

It doesn't make sense to just replace plastic containers with glass, she says, unless those containers are re-used. With sterilising facilities in the shop, bringing a jar back is easy, especially when compared to shipping it overseas after one use to be recycled, as much of Australia's waste cannot be recycled locally.

'Businesses are worried about the extra cost of going plastic-free—but you need to create your own tribe of people who support you by doing whatever it is that will bring them back to your store.

'As businesses we can be leaders, it would be great for the planet.'

Sticking with the big supermarkets

Supermarket shopping can be disheartening if all you can see is plastic packaging. But if you shop carefully, there are still lots of plastic-free choices. Major supermarkets have publicly committed to reducing single-use plastic—which is great news. Meanwhile, use your own string bags or go naked for fruit and veggies, buy in cans and glass jars (and make sure you re-use or recycle them) or buy in paper. Take a close look at some high-volume products like teabags— they may, in fact, be made with synthetic mesh or with paper with plastic additives that don't break down. Most tea brands have this information available online, but it may not be prominent so dig around. Or try searching for plastic-free teabags. Better still, go back to what our grandmas did and use loose leaf tea! On the plus side, it's easy to get some basics in paper or cardboard packages, including flour, eggs, milk, butter, sugar, bicarbonate of soda, cat and dog biscuits, and Epsom salts.

Verdict   You don't need to give up on supermarkets and you can communicate with them via email or social media to encourage changes.

SEARCH TERMS   Q single-use plastics and supermarkets   Q plastic bag ban.

What's in your too-hard basket?

There will always be some things you'd like to buy that can only be found in plastic packaging. You can still make a big difference even if you do buy some of them and recycle the packaging. We've met many people making a huge difference who still haven't entirely broken the plastic habit. It might be those salt and vinegar chips, a favourite cheese, yoghurt or brand of ice cream, or a meal base like tofu. Try to make sure it's a small handbasket, not a shopping trolley.

Safe food storage

Food packaging is a sophisticated and exact science. When you buy perishables like meat, fresh pasta, ready-made meals or fresh vegetables sealed in plastic, suppliers can confidently offer precise use-by dates that extend well beyond the usual shelf life of the products. Why? Because sealed plastic packaging enables storage conditions to be customised based on the best way to delay the spoilage of different kinds of food.

Food goes off because it decays via oxidation (which, for example, turns bananas brown) or the growth of microbes like bacteria, yeast and moulds. To keep food safe and fresh for longer, the challenge is to slow down these processes. Refrigeration works for a few days and freezing can preserve food for months.

But commercial food suppliers can do much more than that with plastic packaging. They can vacuum seal foods, like meat, by sucking out the air, which starves microbes of oxygen and slows oxidation. Or they can use Modified Atmosphere Packaging—this replaces the air inside a sealed pack with precisely calibrated mixes of gases.[7] The best way to keep meat fresh and looking appetising (that is, red) for longer is to use a mix of 70 per cent oxygen (O_2) and 30 per cent carbon dioxide (CO_2). Raw chicken needs 30 per cent CO_2 and 70 per cent nitrogen (N_2) and bread is best with low oxygen to inhibit mould. Even the freshness of fruit and veggies can be extended in a mix of 90 per cent N_2 and five per cent each of O_2 and CO_2.[8]

Packaging is further tweaked using various perforations in the plastic that allow certain gases to be released. This kind of packaging is useful if you want to shop ahead and have food ready in the fridge. (Once the package is open, treat it like fresh food.)

You might recognise some of these:[9]

- Cucumbers—shrink wrap extends shelf life from nine to fifteen days.
- Capsicums—Modified Atmosphere Packaging with perforated plastic film (PP) extends shelf life from four to twenty days.

- Beef—vacuum packaging in oxygen barrier film extends the shelf life from four to 30 days.
- Bananas—in perforated polyethylene (PE) bags shelf life is extended from fifteen to 36 days.

If you are going plastic-free you'll be eating fresh—which is great—but you might also need to think about how you'll manage without extended shelf lives. The easiest option, of course, is shopping regularly and cooking fresh produce within a day or two of purchasing.

You can wrap fruit and veggies in damp tea towels in the crisper and store food in the main body of the fridge using airtight containers. For bread, try wrapping it in a tea towel and storing it in a bread bin or use a reusable bread bag, available online, that's also useful for freezing.

Wrap meat in baking paper before putting it in a container. You could also try preserving meat for longer by marinating it or coating it with cooking oil (cutting off the oxygen to its surface). This method is useful for lots of products—if you have a half-used jar of pesto or tomato paste, for example, cover with a thin film of olive oil. You'll notice any residue above the oil goes mouldy, but what's beneath it stays good. Freezing most foodstuffs is also useful—but always thaw them inside the fridge rather than leaving them on the bench.

Verdict Lots of alternatives to single-use plastic packaging are coming onto the market. These include beeswax wraps, washable reusable silicone (food-grade) cling film and zip-lock bags, metal food storage containers and reusable food-grade plastic containers.

A useful CSIRO guide to safely storing perishable foods can be found on the CSIRO website.[10]

SEARCH TERMS Q plastic-free home/house Q plastic-free storage Q eco food storage Q green food storage Q reusable bread bag.

CHAPTER 6

THE LAUNDRY AND CLEANING

It costs just a few dollars, comes in a (cardboard) box, contains no petrochemicals and can be used to wash or clean just about anything. But most of my generation have never used, or even heard of, Sunlight soap. I only know of its apparent wonders thanks to my grandmothers.

In fact, one grandma, who lives in a modest-sized town in New Zealand, became quite nervous last year during a family visit that coincided with a local shortage of Sunlight soap. With the shelves of all the major stores empty, we eventually snapped up the last box at a convenience store. The shopkeeper immediately regretted letting it go. His own family, too, he said, 'uses it for everything'. Unmoved, we clung like panic-buyers to our purchase. My grandma was relieved; she uses it in the shower, at the basin, at the kitchen sink, to rub on stains before putting clothes into the washing machine— and she swears it keeps her hair baby soft! (My mum, under duress, did give it a go—and says she was surprised to find it is actually pretty good as a shampoo.) Other uses include washing the dog, polishing taps, sinks and shower heads, washing pots and pans and as the base for laundry detergent.[1]

Can we clean without plastic-packaged products?

Yes! It is easy to do without many of those plastic bottles lined up in our laundries and stashed under our sinks. Solid soap is a good place to start. Sunlight, introduced in 1884, was the world's first branded commercial laundry soap. There have, of course, been lots of good soaps released since then that have something wonderful in common— they can be purchased wrapped in paper. You might like Castile soap—made only with vegetable oil, lye (a caustic alkali) and water, plus essential oils for fragrance. Or you might have other personal preferences for soaps that are sulphate- or palm-oil free (Sunlight contains palm oil).

The not too distant past also suggests some other fantastic plastic-free cleaning options. Bicarbonate of soda, also known as bicarb or baking soda (not baking powder), is a cheap, readily available (in cardboard) cleaning base that is useful for just about anything. Lemon juice and white vinegar are also great. And, what about that entirely natural asset, sunshine? The ultraviolent radiation in sunlight works as a natural disinfectant and is powerful enough to kill microbiological pathogens in drinking water (put a clear bottle in sunlight for at least six hours), so drying your laundry in direct sunlight is a very effective, free way of sanitising your wash.[2] (I have not included borax in this list, as it can be very toxic if ingested, especially by children.) And if you look to other cultures you might come across entirely natural soap nuts.

If you prefer to stick with what you know, wander around your local supermarket and shops with a keen eye. You will find some plastic-free gems among the mountains of plastic bottles. Look for things like latex gloves, kitchen wipes made of cellulose, or your favourite commercial washing powder in a cardboard box. You can also look for 100 per cent recycled plastic packaging (and recycle it again) or plant-based plastics. Or buy big, so you have fewer individual containers to dispose of.

WHAT ABOUT GERMS?

If you are worrying around germs, stop! Chances are you don't need costly, plastic-packaged antibacterial products—unless you're a surgeon scrubbing up or a hospital visitor or patient. Numerous studies have found soap and warm water are good enough to kill off about 99 per cent of bacteria.[3] White vinegar, too, is a powerful disinfectant, as are some essential oils. If you still find yourself mesmerised (advertising does work!) by products promising to kill 99.9 per cent of household germs, consider the bigger picture. In much the same way as antibiotics indiscriminately kill off both the good and bad bacteria in our bodies—often leaving only the most virulent, nasty bacteria standing—antibacterial products can also have unintended consequences.

In 2014, the US Food and Drug Administration (FDA) banned triclosan,[4] the key active ingredient in many antibacterial soaps and cleaners and personal-care products like toothpaste. Triclosan was found to be no more effective than soap and water, and there were two more compelling reasons for phasing it out. First, it doesn't kill common viruses, so consumers mistakenly expected protection from colds and flu; and second, the overuse of such agents contributes to antibiotic resistance. According to a 2018 University of Queensland (UQ) study, about 2000 consumer products contain triclosan, many of which are available in Australia and New Zealand. The UQ study warned that its presence in waste water is 'accelerating the spread of antibiotic resistance'.[5] The bottom line: hospital-grade products are great—for hospitals.

NOTE: We do not suggest avoiding products in plastic that are formulated specifically for hospitals and other medical uses and settings.

Here's what we've found works for washing and cleaning. As your store-bought products run out, save spray bottles and other containers to refill.

Washing your clothes

Some commercial **washing powder** brands are available in cardboard boxes, as is **flaked soap** for delicates. If you prefer **liquid detergents**, look for a store that stocks bulk cleaning products and will refill a bottle for you.

Or you can try homemade by grating any soap and mixing it with bicarb soda. I use a ratio of 700 grams of grated soap (five bars or so) to 1 cup of bicarb soda:[6] you can adjust quantities up or down depending on how much you need (or how much grating your arm can cope with). Store the mix in an airtight container. When you have your wash loaded, dissolve a scoop (no precise measuring required) in ½ cup or so of hot water, then add a drop or two of eucalyptus oil and it's ready for use. If you want to make **wool wash**,[7] save up all those annoying little pieces of soap (about a handful's worth) and simmer them in 1½ cups of water, until about 1 cup of liquid is left, then add a drop or two of essential oil. Cool before pouring into a glass jar to store (to be honest, mine solidifies—but I reheat it in the microwave briefly before I use it—or you can dissolve a bit in hot water).

For the ultimate no-plastic environmental wash, you might want to try **soap nuts** (also known as soapberries). These are derived from the plentiful fruit of the *Sapindus* genus of trees, relatives of the lychee, and traditionally are used right across the Indian subcontinent. Once the 'nuts' have been dried, they go into a fabric bag and then in with your wash. The nuts contain saponin which is a surfactant, so they act like soap in your machine. However, in my experience, they work better with hot water than cold. Instead of using a hot cycle, you can soak the bag of soap nuts in boiling water and then pour the liquid into your machine's detergent input. Alternatively, start on a hot cycle to maximise the release of surfactants, then turn your temperature dial to cold after the first few minutes. You can also make a general cleaner by simmering a handful of soap nuts in about 1 litre of water for twenty minutes, then let it cool—handy for everything, including washing the dog and your hair.

Stain removers—These don't only come in plastic bottles! At least one major brand is available in a solid bar. Buy a dish to store your soap, and rub the soap on stains before washing; a little more effort than a spray-on, but a big saving on plastic waste. Otherwise, soaking in bicarb soda works too, or white vinegar for whites.

Pegs and baskets—It's easy to find bamboo, wood and metal pegs, and laundry and washing baskets made of wicker, rattan or other natural materials.

Verdict   There are lots of plastic-free choices for clothes-washing that are cost neutral or even cheaper than their plastic-packaged counterparts and do the job well. It's hard to beat chemical whiteners and stain removers like bleach but there are plenty of good reasons—in addition to plastic packaging—to avoid adding these to our waterways.

SEARCH TERMS   Q soap nuts Q plastic-free home Q plastic-free cleaning Q plastic-free July cleaning.

NOTE: *Synthetic materials shed tiny microplastic fibres when washed, now the single largest source of microplastic pollution. See Chapter 8, The Wardrobe, for further information.*

Washing the dishes

I was thrilled when the bulk store near us introduced refills for **dishwashing liquid**—problem solved. But if this isn't an option, you can try grated soap or bicarb soda in hot water. For pots and pans, make a paste of bicarb soda and white vinegar. Look for **natural bristle dish brushes**, they last much longer and do a much better job than plastic ones. Natural latex (rubber) **gloves** can be found in any supermarket.

For **dishwashers**, some powders are available in cardboard packaging or you can make your own. The easiest option is to use bicarb soda in place of dishwasher powder or tablets and white vinegar as the rinsing agent.

Alternatively, a heavier duty recipe combines 1 cup of bicarb soda with 1 cup of borax and ½ cup of salt.[8] (As my curious and agile nephew is going on two, I don't use borax and I haven't tested this one.) You can also try soap nuts in the dishwasher.

To clean your dishwasher naturally, *Choice* suggests pouring 2 cups of white vinegar into a bowl and putting it on the bottom shelf of your otherwise empty machine (upright, so it doesn't drain out)—run a full cycle but push pause for about 30 minutes mid-cycle to increase soaking time.[9] You can also throw a handful of bicarb soda into an empty dishwasher and run a cycle.

Verdict With a bit of effort and ingenuity you can enjoy the benefits of dishwashers without plastic. It's cost neutral or even cheaper if you go for natural alternatives.

SEARCH TERMS Q dishwasher powder recipes Q eco cleaning Q natural bristle brushes.

Cleaning

It's easy to make your own multipurpose surface cleaner. The base mix is 1 part white vinegar to 3 parts water. One way of improving its cleaning power and bouquet is to add lemon or orange rinds (and let them soak before using) or a few drops of eucalyptus or lavender oil. You can also use dishwashing liquid on a sponge for just about any clean-up. Online stores sell various all-purpose cleaning products in glass jars but think about whether you want to buy and ship heavy containers.

For baths and basins, try mixing bicarb soda with a few drops of eucalyptus or tea tree oil to make a paste. You could also turn back time and use one of the cheap powdered cleansers like Ajax or Bon Ami. These are still on the market and come in a cardboard tube.

What about the toilet? Elbow grease is a good start. Use a **natural bristle brush**, made of something like coconut fibre—a renewable by-product of coconut processing that would otherwise be wasted. You can try adding your bicarb soda paste to the brush. Once that's done, add some white vinegar to the bowl so it fizzes. Your toilet will look and smell very clean. There are also natural toilet bombs (dissolving cubes with a scented bicarb-soda base) on the market that are quick and easy or use, or install.

For mould, white vinegar is also a good bet. A ratio of approximately 80 per cent vinegar to twenty per cent water is strong enough to kill spores, then follow with a bicarb-soda cleaning paste.

Verdict Simplifying cleaning products declutters your cupboards without compromising on cleanliness. Costs vary but there are plenty of affordable options.

SEARCH TERMS 🔍 green cleaning 🔍 eco cleaning 🔍 toilet bombs
🔍 natural spray cleaner 🔍 natural spray and wipe.

Disinfectants

Powerful disinfectants like bleach and ammonia-based products come in plastic, can cause respiratory and skin irritations[10] and are just as harsh on the environment. I grew up without them and lived to tell the tale.

It is hard to go wrong with white vinegar and the science backs this up; it kills about 80 per cent of germs and is also a great deodoriser and grease cutter. And it can combat salmonella, *E. coli* and other resistant 'gram negative' bacteria that cause illnesses like pneumonia, meningitis and other infections.[11] But with far fewer scientific evaluations to date of natural alternatives, it's difficult to compare them.

We all use different ratios of ingredients in homemade products. And while many natural products have useful cleaning and disinfecting properties, that doesn't tell us exactly how to use them. One 2018 study evaluating the microbial properties of nine essential oils found that lemon came out on top and was an effective disinfectant for food preparation surfaces.[12] In 2017 another study concluded citrus (lemon) essential oils were 'natural antimicrobial and antioxidant agents' with potential uses in food systems and the pharmaceutical industry'.[13] Essential oils of orange, thyme, oregano and cinnamon have demonstrated similar antimicrobial properties, as have others such as tea tree and eucalyptus oil.

It's worth learning something about essentials oils and why they work. They've been around for at least 2000 years and are either produced by living organisms or obtained by pressing or distilling plant materials like flowers, buds, seeds, leaves, fruits, roots and barks. To date, we've isolated about 3000 different oils. It's easy to see they are hydrophobic—which just means they repel water, like many other oils. What isn't visible to the human eye—and was only relatively recently described—is that this hydrophobicity means they can also damage the cell membranes of bacteria—a process that triggers leakage from inside the bacteria and then cell death. Yes, it is a bit more complicated than this, but the key point is that essential oils aren't just for hopeful hippies, they are scientifically proven to be effective against many germs.[14] But even though they are entirely natural they are highly concentrated and, like commercial cleaning products, we need to understand how to use them safely. The biggest risk is that young children will taste or drink them—they usually smell great. Also check before using them undiluted on skin; they may cause irritations. If a recipe says to use a few drops, that is all you need! For safety information see: http://healthywa.wa.gov.au/Articles/A_E/Essential-oils.

Lots of research is currently underway, so we'll likely see more and more natural ingredients in scientifically developed products in the future. In the meantime, various useful essential oils come in small glass bottles and a few drops really do go a long way.

NOTE: *Many recipes for homemade cleaning products use borax, but personally I don't because of the risk to small children.*

Verdict It's your home. Plastic packaging may be only one factor among many when it comes to making a personal choice about disinfectants.

SEARCH TERMS Q essential oils and microbial properties Q essential oils for cleaning Q household disinfectants.

Cloths, wipes and brushes

No matter how happy all those TV housewives look as they gaily pull disposable wipes out of plastic packets, I promise you your life will not change if you buy them. However, our environment will. All over the world wet wipes are becoming trapped in sewers where they soak up the oily residue of shampoos, kitchen grease and other gunk washed down our drains to create giant 'fat bergs'. The biggest one ever found—the size of eleven double-decker buses—blocked the London sewerage system in 2017. So, that's a hard no to wet wipes for benches, floors, leather goods, personal care, babies, anything! Even if you don't flush them, they are made of synthetic fibres and come packaged in plastic.

If you look carefully, on some multipurpose **sponge cloths** in supermarkets you'll see a broccoli symbol. Although I doubt they're actually made of this lovely veggie, they are made from plant-derived cellulose. Similar cloths, made in Sweden, are widely available online.

It's also easy to find microfibre cloths that can be used without chemical cleaners. These may be synthetic, but they are long lasting, often come boxed in cardboard and can help you do away with numerous plastic bottles of cleaning products. One line of these cleaning cloths is specifically designed for asthma suffers and will do a great job cleaning all sorts of surfaces using only water, which is great.

Good-quality **natural fibre brooms and brushes** with wooden handles are available online and in stores but may be heavier than their plastic cousins.

Verdict There are lots of great products to choose from at reasonable prices, and cleaning with water only is amazing.

SEARCH TERMS Q eco cleaning cloths Q chemical-free cleaning Q plastic-free cleaning Q natural fibre brushes.

Those other jobs

For tiled or wooden **floors,** use warm water with a little white vinegar and a few drops of essential oil. Alternatively, soap-nut liquid with a couple of drops of tea tree or eucalyptus oil works well and smells great. For **windows and mirrors,** you could try my grandmother's method. Wipe with white vinegar, then with warm water and polish with bunched-up newspaper. I use a microfibre cloth designed for glass and other reflective surfaces and I swear by it. The best thing? You can keep it in the shower and wipe down the glass when you're done. Just about the easiest way to clean I know of.

For **wood** and **leather**, use metal tins of beeswax or other polishes—or, likewise, look for microfibre cloths designed for these jobs.

Verdict Easy and cost-effective. Personally, I don't think anyone needs a huge cupboard full of different cleaning products for every surface or room; simple solutions work everywhere!

SEARCH TERMS Q natural window cleaner Q asthma-friendly cleaning cloths.

Eek—what about plastic bags to line my bin and pick up doggy doo?

The demise of free lightweight plastic bags in 2018 triggered widespread anxiety about our bins and what to do about doggy doo. Bioplastic bags made from corn or other agricultural waste are an emerging alternative, and a wide range of sizes are available (mostly online) for any bin or dog walker.

Note: *If you are buying bags labelled 'biodegradable' this just means they break down into tiny pieces of plastic. Look for 'compostable' bags instead that are derived from plants.*

Verdict Compostable bioplastic bags are not particularly strong but, in my opinion, they are worth it. Save money by using fewer bags—most of your kitchen waste, for example, can be composted. If you are looking for a place to drop off your compost instead of DIY try searching on https://sharewaste.com/share-waste.

SEARCH TERMS Q compostable waste bags Q compostable bin liners.

CHAPTER 7

THE BATHROOM

I have spent the past ten years worrying about my hair—which isn't really that unusual, considering humans have been fussing over hairstyles since about 4000 BC. It's not so much the style I worry about (although I do care), but how to keep my unruly hair *clean*. This began when, at the age of sixteen and largely motivated by a desire to have long hair, I decided to embark on a plastic- and chemical-free hair-care regime.

At the time there wasn't much information out there, and even fewer alternative products. So, after extensive research on a now-defunct web forum called 'long hair journey', I went with the old favourites, bicarb soda for washing my hair and apple cider vinegar as a conditioner. This combination works for many people, but not for me. As I was also swimming regularly in the ocean, my hair soon looked and felt like straw—with the dry, dandruff-y scalp to match. And, despite assurances from the internet that the vinegar smell would dissipate, I found myself walking around school smelling like a pickle factory. It was too much for my teenage vanity and after a few months I gave up. The shower again filled up with plastic bottles.

Later, in my late teens and early twenties, I tried again. This time I went with the 'no poo' method, spurred on by radio discussions about how great your hair would look if you just stopped washing it with shampoo (or poo) and instead rinsed it with clean water. The idea is that our modern cleaning methods strip the hair of natural oils, causing the scalp to compensate by making a whole lot more. By going no poo you restore equilibrium and never have to wash your hair again. Sounds like the dream. But the big challenge for all no poo adherents is the transition period when you look (and smell?) a bit like a greasy, wet rat before your locks return to their soft, bouncy natural state. At least that's what is supposed to happen. I don't doubt the no poo fans and have great respect for those who succeed. But I remained trapped in the purgatory of transition and so abandoned no poo.

More on hair later. This chapter is actually about what you *can* do to use less plastic in the bathroom. There are some quick, easy swaps, but also some challenges. To me, it seems like the plastic bottles, tubes, packets and wrappers in bathrooms multiply like rabbits when you're not paying attention. This is not, perhaps, surprising. Plastic is waterproof, shatterproof, durable and hygienic, just what a damp environment with hard surfaces needs. And personal items like plastic combs and toothbrushes were among the world's first mass-produced plastic consumer goods. But I have often wondered how I could possibly ever have bought (even afforded) so many bottles of various liquids, many of which I didn't even use. Does anyone even remember hair fudge? If so, there's a spare orange bottle languishing at the back of the bathroom cupboard at my parents' place, circa 2005.

Do we really need all this stuff? And how often should we be using it? In 1908 *The New York Times* suggested a good hair wash with soap every four to six weeks.[1] The first liquid shampoo didn't even go on sale until 1914 (the word crept into English in the late 1700s, picked up by British colonists from the Hindu word *champo*, which means 'to press' and refers to a head rub or massage, not a wash). And hair conditioner only came onto the market in the 1970s. Nowadays, 70 per cent of Australians[2] wash their hair every day, despite regular advice columns warning against such over-enthusiasm. By figuring out what you actually need and use, you can stick to the essentials when it comes time to shop.

So, what do we really need in the bathroom? Fortunately, there are a couple of big, easy wins that you can implement straight away. The average Australian household uses $2 worth of toilet paper a week,[3] almost all of which comes plastic-wrapped.[4] The few entirely plastic-free brands aren't hard to find. And for lots of other bathroom stuff it's easy to replace a plastic version with something that does the same thing. And what about all those feminine hygiene products? This unhelpful euphemism suggests we are unhygienic if we don't buy them and obscures just how comfortable, convenient and cheap the alternatives are.

There are also lots of homemade recipes online for the ambitious, many of which are much more sophisticated than my first bicarb soda efforts for hair care. Depending on where you live, there may even be the option to refill old bottles at bulk-purchase stores, with just the kind of products you like to use.

What about plastic microbeads? Fortunately, lots of manufacturers have already committed to phasing them out. If you want to be sure, check the list of ingredients and avoid these plastics: polyethylene (PE), polypropylene (PP), polyethylene terephthalate (PET), polymethyl methacrylate (PMMA), polytetrafluoroethylene (PTFE) and nylon.[5]

How did my hair thing work out? It's still a work in progress. My imperfect solution is to use a solid shampoo bar and to bulk buy conditioner online and eke it out over the year. Another friend has gone for no poo and looks fine, but is a short-haired he.

IMPORTANT NOTE: *We do not recommend avoiding plastics used to package medicines or medical supplies; they are specially designed for keeping medical products/drugs sterile, and for maintaining their effectiveness and longevity. Don't make any changes that could affect your health without seeking medical advice.*

Getting clean (face and body)

When you take a good look at all the getting-clean products on the market, they all boil down (literally, in this case) to the same thing—soap! Soap started life as a solid bar that could be wrapped in paper. There are plenty of wonderful soaps on the market for any type of skin in any kind of fragrance and containing pretty much any kind of oil or moisturiser, including those that are palm-oil free (using something like coconut oil) or made with certified sustainable palm oil. So it's easy to replace plastic and pump bottles of hand wash, body wash, foaming cleanser, liquid soap and so on.

Concerned about sulphates in your soap?

Sulphates are the ingredients in many cleaning and cleansing products that help them foam and lather. But they can cause skin irritation for some people, or you may be like me and find they dry out your skin. Fortunately, there are many sulphate-free products available now and this does extend to soap bars. Just look for 'SLS free' or 'sulphate free' on the (plastic-free) packaging.

What if you don't like soap bars because they, say, go soggy in the shower? Making your own liquid soap from your favourite solid soap can be as easy as taking the production processes back a step. Grate or cut up your soap, dissolve it in warm water, let it sit overnight until it solidifies into a jelly, whizz it up into a liquid using a stick blender, then use to refill a liquid soap dispenser. More complex recipes are available online with things like essential oils.

Verdict Soap, however it starts out, is just soap. Soap bars do a great job and are usually cheaper than their liquid counterparts.

SEARCH TERMS 🔍 soap bars 🔍 sulphate-free soap bars 🔍 DIY liquid soap 🔍 making liquid soap from a bar.

Bath soak

Bath salts have been around forever. They are mostly a combination of ordinary household products like salt, bicarb soda and citric acid with, perhaps, Epsom salts (a mineral compound of magnesium and sulphate—itself a great soak). They are easy to find in the form of paper-wrapped bath bombs. Epsom salts are available in a cardboard box in any supermarket—and the cooled bath water can be bucketed onto the garden as the dissolved magnesium makes for amazing greens! **Bubble baths** are great too—instead of buying big colourful plastic bottles of chemically enhanced liquids, it is easy to find bubble bath bars that you can drop into the water with the same effect.

Oils—A few drops of lavender, rose, neroli or geranium oil are as good as a commercial bath product, with the added benefit of leaving your skin moisturised.

Water-soluble essential oils are the most convenient and are available in glass bottles in the cosmetics aisle of most supermarkets.

Verdict   Bath salts and soaks are one of the easiest switches to make in the bathroom, and they are cheap.

SEARCH TERMS   Q Epsom salts   Q bath bombs   Q bath fizzes Q bath oils   Q bubble bath bars.

Hair care (washing and conditioning)

Honestly, nothing is quite as easy as lathering up with a liquid shampoo and smoothing conditioner through your hair. Glass bottles aren't a great alternative as they're dangerous in the bathroom. But there are plenty of alternatives that are surprisingly effective and cheap. They include:

Back to basics—Use bicarb soda to wash and apple cider vinegar to condition. Mix the bicarb soda with water to make a paste, so it's easier to massage through your hair and scalp. Dilute the apple cider vinegar, about 1 part vinegar to 4 parts water, and rinse for soft, smooth hair. (The vinegar rinse removes built-up residue from commercial products too.)

Homemade shampoos—There are lots of recipes online, all of which are based on the basic premise of a cleanser (soap) and a moisturiser (something like coconut oil).

Shampoo and conditioner bars—These are pretty much what you might imagine: a solid version of both shampoo and conditioner that work well and come in cardboard or paper. As with hair-care products in plastic bottles, check the list of ingredients if you don't want ingredients like sulphates. There is, for example, a great Tasmanian company that's entirely plastic-free (and has been for 25 years) and a newer entrant to this growing market from New Zealand. They make excellent shampoo and conditioner bars.

No poo—This method involves rinsing your hair under pretty hot water and 'scritching' your scalp—basically a form of vigorous massage—to move the oils down the hair shaft. It can take anywhere from a few weeks to a few months for your oil production to level out. This method works best for shorter hair.

Coconut oil conditioner—Some people use pure coconut oil as a conditioner. It is widely available in tins or glass jars.

For a while, I used coconut oil as a deep conditioning mask on my hair. My hair was very shiny, but I also ended up with teenage-esque breakouts on my back.

Buy in bulk—If you just can't give up on your favourite hair-care products, don't! Try to reduce their plastic footprint instead. Contact the manufacturer direct and ask them about alternatives, such as refilling your own containers or buying in bulk, so you can decant into your own smaller containers for use. Buying in bulk often ends up cheaper. If using your products straight from the big bottles, be aware that we usually over-pour when we have lots of something. If you don't want to buy in bulk yourself, some bulk stores are offering a limited range of liquid shampoos and conditioners. Just bring your own bottles and refill.

Verdict   Like a lot of things in the bathroom, hair care is pretty personal. Give a few things a try and see what works best for you, your hair and your lifestyle. Costs are variable, depending on what you like.

SEARCH TERMS   Q no poo method   Q shampoo alternatives Q conditioner alternatives   Q natural hair care   Q bicarb soda for hair   Q vinegar for hair   Q shampoo recipes   Q shampoo bars   Q conditioner bars.

Scrubs and exfoliants

Physical exfoliants, like body scrubs with grainy textures, can leave you feeling incredibly clean and refreshed, but most come in plastic tubes. It's also tricky to be sure they don't contain plastic microbeads; these are banned in New Zealand, but Australia relies on a voluntary industry phase-out. The good news is it's quick and easy to make your own scrubs with ingredients from your kitchen cupboard.

The most basic scrub for body or face involves mixing 1 part oil with 1 part sugar. I've road-tested this recipe and can report it leaves your skin feeling super smooth and hydrated. You will probably want to customise it, depending on whether you are using it on your face or body. For my face, I use really fine sugar, usually castor sugar, and an oil that I've tested and that works for me, like jojoba or almond oil. As the skin on your body is less sensitive—and less liable to break out—you can use cheaper options like olive oil and coarser sugar, such as raw sugar. Coconut oil make me break out, so I don't use it, but many people swear by it. You can also add essential oils to this basic scrub.

A few scrubs containing bamboo granules or ground apricot kernels or other natural ingredients can be found in glass pots.

When it comes to exfoliating with plastic sponges and loofahs, replace them with natural bristle wooden body brushes and jute, hemp and sisal sponges.

Verdict   Scrubs and exfoliants are cheap and easy.

SEARCH TERMS   Q homemade face and body scrub   Q plastic-free exfoliants.

Deodorant—Improving

Most commercial deodorants come in aluminium spray cans or, for roll-ons, glass or plastic tubes. Glass or metal bases can be easily recycled, but nearly all deodorants also have a plastic spray nozzle or a plastic roller top. Instead try:

Paste deodorants—These natural alternatives are available from health-food stores or can be ordered online. They come in glass jars or metal tins and are applied with small metal spatulas or your fingers.

Solid deodorant bars—These are similar to paste deodorants, but are in a solid form.

Homemade deodorant—Bibcarb soda, one of the most versatile substances on earth it seems, again stars as the key ingredient. To make deodorant, it's mixed with arrowroot or cornstarch, something to make it sticky and spreadable like shea butter, plus a nice essential oil to keep you smelling fresh. Lots of different recipes are available online.

Verdict Natural deodorants will stop you smelling, but they aren't antiperspirants so they won't stop you sweating (commercial products have ingredients like aluminium and other chemicals to do this part of the job). I haven't tried making my own, but the paste I buy online smells great. I do use a commercial antiperspirant (in a glass roll-on) if I have an important occasion that would go better without sweat rings.

SEARCH TERMS 🔍 natural deodorant 🔍 deodorant recipe 🔍 DIY deodorant.

Toilet paper

Look for brands made from recycled paper that come wrapped in paper, not soft plastic. Some supermarkets stock paper-wrapped brands, plenty more are available online.

Verdict Paper-wrapped toilet paper is just the same on your bum! Prices are also comparable.

SEARCH TERMS   Q recycled toilet paper   Q no-plastic toilet paper
Q tree-free toilet paper.

Menstrual products

It's hard to imagine we're in the grip of a revolution in the menstrual products market when you wander down supermarket aisles; all you see are shelves piled high with bright (pink) plastic-wrapped packages of disposable sanitary pads and tampons, with various flowery names and discreet product descriptions.

Beyond the big stores, however, it's a different story. Reusable, plastic-free menstrual products are exploding in popularity online—with more and more women choosing to switch. From menstrual cups to period panties, these options offer the same convenience as conventional products—but as they are reusable we can save money and the environment at the same time.

Menstrual cups—They're soft, flexible medical-grade silicon cups that fit over the cervix to catch up to twelve hours of flow, so you don't have to empty them in public toilets. They are easy to wash out and sterilise. Several reputable brands are available online and one major Australian chemist chain recently put them on the shelves. There are different sizes available to suit your flow and whether or not you've given birth.

Washable pads—These are colourful or neutral undyed pads that look like conventional disposable pads but can be washed and re-used. Made of layers of highly absorbent fabric, with a leakproof backing, some are 100 per cent cotton. Like disposable pads, they're available in overnight, super, regular, light and for light bladder leakage, and can be used to back up menstrual cups.

Period panties—These are underwear with a pad and leak-proof barrier incorporated into the crotch. Wear like regular underwear during your period. Rinse after use, then just pop them in the wash.

Sponges—Harvested natural sea sponges can be used like tampons. Look for them online.

Compostable, plastic-free pads and tampons—Available in Australia and NZ online, these are currently imported and cost more than plastic-based products.

PLASTIC-FREE PERIODS

Only 100 years ago, my great-grandmother ran off and hid in the bush when her first period started, terrified she was bleeding to death. No one had ever told her about periods. It was only when she was found by her older sister that she was let in on the secret and was assured that she would survive! The taboo in those days was such that her mother and sisters had kept menstruation hidden, even in their crowded farmhouse where the ten siblings often had to share beds.

At the time, periods were mostly managed by stuffing rags in your underwear—and a lot of discreet washing. This inconvenience and shame kept women close to home during their 'monthlies'. By the 1930s, however, an American actress, Mrs Leona W. Chalmers,[6] had come up with a solution. She patented an ingenious flexible rubber 'cup' that could be fitted inside the vagina to create a seal over the cervix. This allowed her to go out confidently onto the stage every night, without worrying about her flow. Alas, this was a bit too much for public discussion in an era when people were still adjusting to the idea of women wearing trousers. Mrs Chalmers' menstrual cup was mostly forgotten.

I am glad to say it's back. Since 2002 menstrual cups made from medical-grade silicon have been available online, and other reusable products have followed. I find a cup much more convenient and comfortable than I ever found tampons or pads. And there are many other good reasons to try them and all the other reusable products out there.

First, every woman uses 10,000–16,000[7] disposable sanitary products over their lifetime, which translates into hundreds of kilograms of waste to landfill or hundreds of thousands of used items in our waterways if they are flushed (as they often are). In the UK a 2016 clean-up recorded twenty tampons and sanitary items per 100 metres of shoreline.[8]

Second, pads are up to 90 per cent plastic.[9] As most brands are a mix of fossil fuel–derived low-density polyethylene (LDPE), cotton and plastic, they take 500–800 years to break down when dumped. Many tampons also contain synthetic fibres. And, although some tampons are cotton, cotton is a water and energy-intensive crop. *Choice* recently rated reusable menstrual products as having 'minimal environmental impact' compared to tampons and pads.

Third, when products are disposable we have to buy them over and over again. Unsurprisingly, menstrual cups aren't stocked by most of the big stores that prefer to get repeat sales.

Verdict I think a menstrual cup is the most liberating device a woman can own! It's comfortable, works well, there's no ongoing cost—and it's easy to keep clean. For me, this convenience is important and has deterred me from both washable pads and period panties. That said, I have friends who haven't taken to the menstrual cup and swear by period pants.

SEARCH TERMS 🔍 menstrual cup 🔍 washable cloth pads 🔍 plastic-free periods 🔍 less-plastic periods 🔍 reusable sanitary products.

Toothbrushes

About 4.7 billion plastic toothbrushes wash up on the world's shores every year, so it's worth finding an alternative. Bamboo-handled toothbrushes are an improvement, but they still have nylon bristles. Cut or pull the bristles out (they have to go to landfill) before disposing of the handles in the compost.

Verdict Okay, but all seem to be designed with a strangely small cleaning head, so they take a little getting used to. Prices comparable to plastic products.

SEARCH TERMS 🔍 bamboo toothbrush 🔍 plastic-free health and beauty.

Toothpaste

Commercial toothpaste seems to come in plastic in Australian and New Zealand, or plastic/metallic tubes with plastic lids. Glass jars are available in Europe, so may be coming here soon.

Make your own—Loads of recipes are available online, but the main ingredients are usually bicarb soda, coconut oil, a sweetener (stevia, for example), flavour or essential oil and water. Pretty easy if you have the time.

Tablets—Another option is to buy toothpaste tablets that are crushed in the mouth and mixed with saliva to form a paste for brushing. They are available in metal tins from some cosmetic retailers.

Verdict The taste of bicarb soda isn't easy to mask, but both homemade toothpaste and tablets are okay and the aftertaste is clean. Remember there is no fluoride in homemade toothpaste. Alternatively, discuss toothpaste with your dentist. The cost of homemade is negligible.

SEARCH TERMS 🔍 toothpaste recipes 🔍 DIY toothpaste 🔍 make your own toothpaste.

Dental floss

As dental floss is, basically, a plastic string—and as many natural fibres just break—what do we do? Fortunately, some innovative individuals have come up with a nice-tasting bamboo version (a Queensland product) and a silk version. Look online but expect to pay more than for plastic. And, there's always the cheap back-to-basics option: toothpicks!

Verdict   My personal choice is to brush carefully and, if necessary, use a bamboo toothpick.

SEARCH TERMS   Q plastic-free shopping and dental floss
Q bamboo dental floss   Q silk dental floss.

Shaving

Shaving has been around for much, much longer than disposable razors, and people managed to get a close shave without plastic. We don't need to go back as far as a Sweeney Todd folding razor (otherwise known as the cut-throat), but the stainless-steel safety razor is a great replacement. It lasts forever, and the blades can be sharpened, changed, then recycled.

You could also go for an electric razor that, likewise, lasts and lasts, if you look after it.

For shaving foam, look for a paper-wrapped stick, or use soap. For a brush, look for an old barber style, with natural bristles and a wooden or ceramic handle. These are increasingly popular and can be found in stores and online.

Verdict   Safety razors are easy to use and are much cheaper in the long run than constantly having to replace disposable razors.

SEARCH TERMS   Q manual shaving   Q traditional barber sets Q shaving sets   Q stainless-steel razor.

Moisturisers

Has there ever been a product that promised us so much? Wrinkle-busting, anti-aging, gravity-defying, oh, and collagen-boosting! Unfortunately, the majority of them come in small plastic tubes and tubs that clutter up our shelves and landfill.

Do you need it? Do you really need different bottles for your face, hands and body? Experiment and see if one product can be used all over. For your body, some oils, like coconut oil or shea butter, can replace moisturiser and usually come in glass bottles. Or look for your favourite products in recyclable metal pots or tubes—some brands are making moisturisers available in metal, glass or ceramic pots. Though these tend to be expensive.

Solid bars—More and more companies are making solid moisturiser bars, for both face and body, that you warm in your hands and rub on.

Make your own—Basic ingredients are oil, beeswax and essential oils. I haven't been game to try this yet, but the recipes look straightforward.

Verdict A very personal category, and what works for you depends on so many things—including your skin type, age, budget and how much time you have to experiment on alternatives. I haven't yet given up my face cream (which does come in plastic), but I don't use body moisturiser for most of the year. Like moisturisers in plastic packaging, you can spend as much or as little as you like.

SEARCH TERMS Q plastic-free moisturisers Q plastic-free creams.

A PLASTIC-FREE PIONEER

As a teenager, Jill Saunders craved all those shiny plastic tubes of wonder products that promised to banish adolescent pimples. But she also had life-long eczema, and commercial creams and lotions just made it worse.

The solution was to go back to her grandmother's natural remedies. And Jill was so successful in curing her own skin woes that she continued to test and develop new recipes until she'd come up with a range of organic skin, beauty and hair products, many using olive oil, beeswax and Tasmanian leatherwood honey. Their point of difference wasn't just natural ingredients—they were entirely plastic-free.

This meant making shampoos, conditioners and moisturisers as solid bars sold in cardboard packaging—something unfamiliar to consumers used to big plastic bottles of liquids.

'They weren't, in fact, new inventions,' Jill says of her shampoo bars, the first on the Australian market.

'My grandmother would use leftover fat to make handmade soap and shampoo bars when I was growing up—that we used for just about everything.

'So, I just returned to that idea of something that was natural, plastic-free and biodegradable.'

Her business Beauty and the Bees (www.beebeauty.com.au) has now been trading entirely plastic-free for 25 years.

'I did a lot of research when I was starting out and realised plastics leaked dioxins during manufacture, leaked phthalates into things we use and are made of oil; I didn't want to be part of them going to landfill.'

That's not to say it's been easy. Without cheap plastics, it's been harder to compete on price against the rise of organic personal care products worldwide. And when Jill added creams to her range she used glass jars, which are heavy and can be challenging to ship to a global customer base.

'Worldwide, there are millions of organic, chemical-free products on the market that come in containers made from petrochemicals, which doesn't really make sense to me.'

And as organic ingredients are relatively expensive, it takes a shift in consumer behaviour—away from the assumption that bigger is better—to choose smaller quantities of a natural product over, say, bargain plastic pump packs.

Recently, Jill says, she noticed a perceptible shift. There's not just interest in natural products, but also in what they come packaged in.

In her own life, she has long avoided plastics as her own skin problems vanished when she divested herself of commercial personal-care and home-cleaning products. But it's not an absolute.

'The most practical advice I could give is to never buy something in a container that can't be re-used or refilled—you'll just have to throw it out.'

Sunscreen

Don't get burnt because you can't find a sunscreen that is not packaged in plastic. Keep using sunscreen if you need it, especially given the high UV index in Australia and New Zealand. You can, of course, also wear long-sleeved shirts, rash vests and hats to stay sun safe.

A handful of plastic-free products are available online, including a natural sunscreen stick that looks like a big lip balm and comes in a cardboard tube. I have not found any of these products on sale in Australia or New Zealand, but some of you may be more skilled 'Googlers' than I am.

Verdict   Very challenging, but hopefully manufacturers will catch up with consumer demand as sunscreen isn't something we can make at home!

SEARCH TERMS   🔍 natural sunscreen   🔍 plastic-free sunscreen.

Make-up

As someone whose make-up use is limited to vaguely smearing tinted moisturiser on my face each morning, I am not really qualified to comment. It's also a very personal issue. There are some innovative options out there like Biome's Beauty Bars in Brisbane, which sell naked ingredients for skin-care and cleaning products. The ingredients are also available online. There are also thousands of recipes online for everything from mascara to face powder.

When it comes to applying and removing make-up, swap plastic-mounted cotton buds for bamboo cotton buds, and polyester make-up wipes for reusable cotton make-up pads or muslin cloths.

Verdict   More effort required if you want to reduce the plastic footprint of your make-up. Alternatively believe in yourself—you probably look fine without too much cover-up!

SEARCH TERMS   🔍 plastic-free make-up   🔍 naked make-up   🔍 natural make-up   🔍 Biome.

CHAPTER 8

YOUR WARDROBE

I have spent far too many years in retail therapy. For as long as I can remember, going shopping for clothes was my generation's social go-to and the cure-all for just about any problem. My groaning wardrobe, however, feels more like a persistent hangover (financial and otherwise). I know there is help out there, if I only I would take it. If I followed the advice of the Japanese decluttering guru Marie Kondo, I would be placing my hand on every single item of clothing and inquiring as to whether it brings me joy. As it likely doesn't, I'd be tossing most of it out. But then I'd just be adding to the huge glut of perfectly usable clothes going into landfill, the bulk of which contain synthetic fibres made from petroleum. Synthetics are plastics too, and are just as hard on the environment as plastic packaging.

So, I have a better idea. As my goal is to avoid plastic, I should be putting my hand—mindfully—on potential purchases while they are still in the shops. Then I might have a reasonable chance of not buying them in the first place. I might, in fact, finally learn the lesson my mum has preached all my life. She is someone who believes that if you buy well, you only buy once. She has, at times, taken this to extremes. She kept jeans from her uni days, then her corporate pants and skirt suits (only quality fabrics, of course, she insists) from the 1980s and '90s, as well as special things like lovely handknitted jumpers made by family members; all too good to throw away. I was slow to appreciate this approach. Funnily enough, she was right. High-waisted jeans came back into fashion briefly at exactly the right time for me to wear her beloved old uni jeans—to uni. Definitely a way to waste not, want not. Not, however, always a strategy for getting your photo in the fashion blogs (unless you can carry off shoulder pads and are willing to wait the 30 or so years for them to be cool again).

Getting back to the point, I am not surprised that my tween then teen shopping binges coincided with the doubling of global clothing textile and footwear production from 2000 to 2014 and the arrival of fast fashion. Like fast food, fast fashion is initially alluring.[1] We flocked to malls. We felt like kids in a soft-play plastic-ball pit, surrounded by colourful fun. Fast fashion is designed to be worn ten times or less before moving on to the next new look, so it must be competitively priced. Not quite single-use disposable. But what about a $2 T-shirt? Why bother washing it, if you can just throw it out and get another one? Fast fashion has created a huge increase in demand for cheap synthetic fabrics and blends that are, like other plastics, petroleum based. And, like single-use plastics, fast fashion is easy to buy but hard to (sustainably) dispose of properly. Almost one in five of all garments made today will be left unworn, or barely used; that's a billion pieces of clothing we didn't really want, let alone need.[2] The clothing, textiles and footwear industries are the second-biggest polluters on the planet, after oil refining. In the UK, consumers spend US$66 billion on their wardrobes a year; yet consumers have an estimated US$47.6 billion worth of unworn clothes still sitting in their wardrobes.[3]

I don't want to sound alarmist, but there's more. Synthetic textiles shed plastic microfibres when washed. They're everywhere. They've been found embedded in the lining of the gastrointestinal tracts of fish all over the world.[4] They're in our drinking water and our ecosystems (I'll get back to this).

The good news is that there are lots of people innovating in this space. Did you know you can buy garments made entirely from recycled PET water bottles or new bioplastic fabrics made from things like pineapple, and mushrooms? H&M, for example, has turned 100 million or so drink bottles into recovered synthetics. In 2018, Adidas sold one million pairs of trainers[5] made from recycled ocean plastics (although to put that in perspective, they sold 402 million pairs made from virgin resources). The fashion industry itself is also aware consumers want it to lift its environmental game. An international industry magazine recently confessed to putting off discussing sustainability as its own primary function is to give 'its [industry] readers advice on how to sell more'.[6] However, it conceded: 'The only way to act or be sustainable—in no matter what industry or area—is by producing, selling and consuming less. Way less. It is as simple as that.'

Putting the brakes on fast fashion

We hear a lot about retail sales figures on the news. If they're up or growing, we are buoyed by economic confidence. If they're down or slowing, we worry the sky is about to fall in. That can make it tricky to advocate buying fewer clothes and other plastic consumer items, and hanging onto them for longer. Shouldn't we be out there spending, doing our bit for the economy? Yes and no. It is true that we need money to circulate and that spending creates jobs. But we don't have to spend it on stuff; how about using the money you save on buying less fast fashion to fund some experiences instead.

If you have a massage, or see a band, or go to the theatre, you are still contributing to the economy, just not its plastic footprint (so long as you don't match the outing with fast food in disposable plastic containers). There's also much to be said for buying more expensive, better-quality clothes—made of natural fibres—that will last. Sometimes paying more for less can be a good buy.

ADVICE FROM A MASTER SHOPPER

I don't feel qualified to give anyone fashion advice, and you already know why I won't ask my mum. But my younger sister, Elowyn (our illustrator), is a better bet for a few reasons. First, she did a degree in design (so she is supposed to know what looks good) and, second, she's been a pretty hardcore plastic avoider for quite a while. And, as a 23-year-old design graduate on the internship circuit, she has lots of experience in stretching her (few) dollars a long way. Here is her purchasing approach.

Step 1: Adopt a shopping philosophy and stick to it. Go for quality over quantity, and longevity and durability over a short-term flurry of Instagram likes. This can be harder than it might seem if you are accustomed to coming home with lots of bags and pawing over them gleefully.

The core idea is to buy much less and to use it for much longer. You need to decide what quality means to you, so you'll value your purchases. Good classic designs and good-quality construction and fabrics add up to something that will last and will hold their shape.

Then make sure you really like it and that it suits your body type. Go for a comfortable, not an aspirational fit. If we're honest, we'd admit we buy clothes that other people will admire. If you choose a timeless style that's flattering on you, rather than the latest fashion fad, you'll get noticed for many years to come. That's a better outcome than a one-season wonder that looks dated within six months. Try not to be dazzled by the season's latest colours—remember fluoro colours have been in fashion, too. If you stick to basic colours, you can brighten up outfits with accessories.

Step 2: Get onto 'goodonyou'—the Fashion without Harm app—or a similar website or app. Find out what brands are good for the environment and locate stores near you. These apps can also help you make decisions about online purchases. Make a resolution—maybe no brands below four stars. Then stick to it. **goodonyou. eco/app/**

Step 3: Prevaricate! Take ages deciding on your purchases and talk incessantly to family members and friends about your various options, not forgetting to show them lots of websites! Even if they do eventually get annoyed, don't worry, it's part of turning clothes from a throw-away impulse buy into an important investment decision.

Step 4: Recruit your friends to do pretty much the same (yes, you'll have to listen to them, too). This isn't just good for the planet. It means that if you want a break from your own classic wardrobe, you can swap it for someone else's quality clothes, either short or long term.

Step 5: Use all the free time you have now you're not constantly shopping to visit markets, small designers' and craft shops, and second-hand shops. They're filled with accessories and scarves that can also be shared and swapped for variety. You can wear a pair of good black jeans for years—in fact, until they fall apart—if you have just one item, like a big pair of earrings or a colourful top, to change the look.

What comes out in the wash

A lot! Every time you put a piece of clothing through a machine cycle it sheds thousands of microfibres. As many of these are too small to be filtered out, they end up in waterways and oceans. Synthetics, which make up the bulk of our clothes these days, are shedding plastic microfibres that aren't biodegradable and can act as magnets for dangerous pollutants like heavy metals and various nasty microbes.[7] There's growing evidence these tiny plastic fibres are being ingested by marine life and are seeping into our ecosystems and the food chain. Based on calculations by the University of California, a city the size of Sydney is flushing plastic microfibres equivalent to 7.5 million plastic shopping bags down our drains via our washing machines every single day. For Auckland, it's about 2.1 million plastic bags' worth a day. Sydney-based ecologist Dr Mark Browne, who discovered the link between plastic microfibre pollution and our laundries in 2011, found synthetic clothing is the single largest source of microplastics in our waterways. But what are we doing about it?

We don't yet know enough about what fabrics shed the most fibres and why—and how they then impact on ecosystems and human health. Dr Browne says medical evidence shows that when microplastics transfer into human tissue they can cause inflammation and fibrosis,[8] but there is much more we need to find out. Meanwhile, some potential solutions are coming onto the market, like the Guppyfriend wash bag that traps fibres—wash your synthetic clothes in it, then scrape out the fibres and put them in the bin—and the Cora Ball, designed so fibres stick to it in the washing machine. Front loader washing machines also seem to generate fewer microfibres than top loaders. However, there's not yet enough peer-reviewed evidence to conclude that any of these options work.

But there is a lot of research underway worldwide. At the University of New South Wales, Dr Browne's team is working on scientifically verified methods to avoid and intercept microfibres. They are also comparing the fibre emissions of natural and plastic fibres and different clothing brands and investigating how well various washing machine filters work.

And there's always that old-fashioned solution: wash less. To my grandmother, clothes were never just clean or dirty, there was much in between, including those handy half-dirty clothes you could get away with wearing again without offending your friends.

Verdict First take a deep breath! This is not good news, but it's not unsurmountable either. Why not follow this evolving debate; clothes shopping will be more interesting!

SEARCH TERMS   Q plastic microfibres   Q Guppyfriend   Q Cora Ball   Q microfibre pollution.

The fabric conundrum—what will I wear?

It's not just *what will I wear?*, but *what will it be made of?*
Comparing synthetic fabrics to natural alternatives isn't as
straightforward as it might seem. Synthetics are especially
problematic because they are derived from petroleum, shed
harmful plastic fibres and are not routinely recycled. But
natural fibres aren't all benign either. Here's some information to help you decide.

Synthetics

Scientists have been making synthetic fabrics in labs for
about a century. Rayon and nylon were early alternatives
to silk, then polyester burst onto the market in the 1950s.
That's when we discovered the joys of wash and wear.
Synthetics freed us from the laborious washing, starching
and ironing of cottons of the past. They were also cheap
and warm and could be layered to regulate temperature.
Instead of heavy, stiff leather and wool, which can absorb
moisture out in the bush or the snow, synthetics also gave
us all kinds of lightweight warm clothes, plus breathable
waterproofing with fabrics like Gore-Tex. This enabled
the outdoor apparel market to take off. The addition of

stretch fabrics like Lycra and Spandex introduced us—for better or for worse—to active wear!

About 60 per cent of fabrics currently used in garment manufacturing are synthetic, dominated by polyester. With fantastic advances in polymer chemistry, synthetic fabrics can be pretty much anything we want; they can drape like silk, wick moisture away from our skin at the gym and provide comfy stretch in our jeans.

Verdict   Synthetics do the job well, but their environmental cost is becoming apparent.

SEARCH TERMS   🔍 synthetic fabrics   🔍 polyester   🔍 Gore-Tex   🔍 Lycra.

Renewable and recycled fabrics

It might seem difficult to live without synthetics but there are an increasing number of alternatives on offer.

Cotton—the most widely used fabric worldwide after synthetics—is great to wear and can be long lasting. But there's lots to consider. One T-shirt takes 500 litres (at least five full bathtubs) of water to produce using cotton grown in irrigated fields. And it takes 11,000 litres of water for every kilogram of finished cotton clothing. About 2.5 per cent of agricultural land worldwide is used to grow cotton, but the industry accounts for 24 per cent of global insecticide use.[9] You could go for rain-fed organic cotton that uses less water and no chemicals.

Denim—This is produced from cotton via a harsh, chemical-heavy process. One interesting tip: some people claim jeans can be worn unwashed for months (putting them in the freezer to eliminate smells), saving on energy and water![10]

Bamboo—This textile uses much less water than cotton, doesn't need pesticides and is harvested at the base of the plant, allowing it to regrow. It is increasingly used for baby and kids wear, underwear and other garments needing soft fabrics. As bamboo groves regenerate quickly, they are also useful in fixing carbon from the atmosphere. But its success has sparked fears too much land will be cleared in China for commercial production, threatening panda habitat. It can also be more expensive than synthetics or cotton.

Merino wool—Wool can compete with synthetics in almost all categories, including outdoor and active wear and even underwear, as there have been huge advances in spinning

HOW ABOUT WEARING OCEAN TRASH, FRUIT OR EVEN MILK?

When my parents got married, my dad wore a pineapple shirt. Not a gaudy Hawaiian shirt with pineapples on it, but a beautiful, fine cream embroidered shirt that's used for formal occasions in the Philippines (where he was born). The Filipinos have been extracting the fibres of pineapple leaves for centuries, which is a smart use of the huge volumes of waste left over after the pineapples are harvested. I might be exaggerating, but apparently their fibres are as creamy and lustrous as silk and good for hand weaving into delicate pina cloth, which is used to make garments you keep for a lifetime.

More recently, Pinatex, a super sustainable industrial pineapple fabric, has hit the global market. It's a bit like faux leather or synthetic plastic and is useful for wallets, shoes and bags and even upholstery and interior furnishings. Mushrooms are also proving useful for faux leather, or vegan leather as it is often called. Many other natural fibres are being revived for textiles, like banana waste fibres, kapok (a sub-tropical tree), nettles and lotus stems; all of which date back

thousands of years. Then there's also a new generation of textiles made from the used coffee grounds
cafes throw away.

Before industrialisation, fibres were sourced from
plants or animals. Animal fibres are proteins; you might
recall being promised miracles by hair-care products
containing keratin, which just means you're putting a
fibrous protein from waste hair (probably a sheep's)
back into your hair! It turns out milk also contains
useful protein fibres.[11] They've recently been turned
into one of the most innovative new fabrics around—
Qmilch.[12] The fabric was developed in Germany when a
microbiology student realised huge volumes of unused
sour milk were going to waste. So, it has been turned
into a mindboggling range of biopolymers from silky
fabrics to yarn, felt and even a natural make-up base.
Like all wool-based fibres, QMilch can be composted,
even at home.

But perhaps the current hero products in the
waste-not clothing category are garments made
from ocean trash. Along with the Adidas Ocean Parley
shoe range, H&M last year launched a collection of
gowns made from Bionic, a fabric range developed
using recovered plastic pollution from the oceans and
shorelines. Another innovation, Econyl, replaces virgin

nylon and is made from old fishing nets—one of the biggest sources of ocean plastics—and other waste.

The outdoor clothing company Patagonia began making garments from recycled soft-drink bottles back in 1993. It now has collections filled with recycled waste and is happy to take its own worn-out garments back. Kathmandu, another outdoor clothing company, uses seventeen recycled plastic bottles in a backpack, fifteen in a fleece jacket and six in a T-shirt. Or you could look for active wear from the Girlfriend Collective, which uses fabrics made from plastic bottles recycled in Taiwan—one nation that is solving its waste crisis by turning garbage into useful products.

I think it's great to make footwear and clothing out of ocean waste—but it may still release plastic microfibres that will find their way back into waterways and oceans.

and manufacturing technologies since the days of damp handknits. Great gym wear made of ultrafine merino is available, including one range that uses biosynthetic elastic made from wood fibre. One big advantage with wool active wear is that it doesn't smell! Outdoor clothing brands also have lots of merino options—including quick-dry layers—and major fashion brands usually have some merino items. Merino clothes are not cheap, but they are lovely to wear and very durable.

Hemp—This plant is better known for its use in ropes and, well, for cannabis production. Its fibre is, however, also useful for clothing and its production uses about one-fifth of the water required for cotton. Hemp clothing still has a hippy image but is fine to wear and often inexpensive.

Silk—Woven into fabrics to dress Chinese empresses for almost 5000 years, it is an entirely natural product and feels and looks great. But silk is often not popular with vegans as those millions of caterpillars—raised for their sole party trick of spinning silk cocoons—are gassed or boiled alive. However, vegan silk is available—a modified process lets the moths emerge alive before the cocoon is taken. Silk is expensive, vegan silk is even more expensive.

Tencel (or lyocell)—It might sound very much like lots of synthetics, but don't be confused by the name! It's a bio-synthetic made from the wood pulp of eucalyptus trees.[13] Tencel production uses much less land and water than cotton growing, and the chemicals used in processing are recovered. Expensive! It gets some rave reviews on the internet, but I haven't tried it.

Verdict   A personal opinion: I prefer natural fabrics!

SEARCH TERMS   Q organic fabrics   Q sustainable textiles   Q natural fabrics   Q organic clothing   Q sustainable textile innovation   Q slow fashion   Q sustainable style   Q fashion for good.

CHAPTER 9

PLASTIC-FREE KIDS

Never take advice on parenting from someone who hasn't raised kids themselves. Particularly those pesky 'I am an involved auntie or uncle types' who go on and on. Which is me. So, although I have two nephews and a niece (who I probably should call adorable in case they read this later), I am entirely unqualified to suggest anything to anyone who is actually doing the real job of parenting, particularly if you're parenting toddlers (I do know this much, as my niece and one of my nephews are both two and I have seen them in action). So, it's not really up to me to point out that a single adult throws away an average of

329 plastic items a year, a couple 658, but a family of four uses an average of 2764 items, according to a UK study.[1] But I will. In case the maths isn't obvious, this means we somehow generate over twice as much plastic rubbish as soon as we have kids.

To overcome my lack of credentials, I have recruited my older sister, Prema, mother of a very cute two-year-old Energiser bunny; my mother, who brought up five of us, and, in the research stage, my grandmother, who had four kids, and even remembered life before plastic.

Before I hand over to people who know better, can I just say one thing? Please, please, please do not buy your darling a babyccino in a non-recyclable, plastic-lined cup with a plastic straw sticking out of it to hold the marshmallow—all this rubbish will last hundreds of years in the environment, but only a few minutes in your child's life. I mean never, ever, but especially not every day. Get them a small KeepCup or similar in funky colours that they can own, look after and enjoy. Oh, and just one more thing. Please, please refuse balloons, always. The CSIRO found they are in the top three waste items for harming wildlife: their bright colours mean they are confused with food.[2] I'd prefer today's kids to inherit something better than a plasticised planet.

IS PLASTIC BAD FOR BABIES AND TODDLERS?

Plastic is not necessarily bad for children. However, babies and children are more vulnerable to the chemical additives in some plastics that have been found to disrupt the human endocrine system. These include Bisphenol A (BPA), which is linked to a long list of diseases. BPA has been removed from most baby bottles and toys, but there are still questions about the additives that have replaced it. Other plastics like cling film and some food packaging still contain known endocrine-disrupting chemicals. As *Choice* reported (see Chapter 2, Good Plastic, Bad Plastic), these can leach into food, so it's worth checking if the food you are feeding your children is affected. *Choice* suggests plastics number 3 and number 7 are the ones to avoid.[3]

Getting off to a plastic-free start

In their natural state, before they are packaged up neatly in disposable nappies and cute outfits, babies and toddlers are messy. The magic of disposable nappies, which draw moisture away from delicate skin and feature leak guards, has transformed early parenting. Ditto, wet wipes. These are truly amazing products . . . for parents. But both disposable nappies and wet wipes contain mountains of plastic fibres. It takes about 1 cup of crude oil to make just one disposable nappy, and Australians and New Zealanders use about 3.75 million of them a day. In landfill, where they mostly end up, they take about 150 years to break down.[4] In the environment, well, use your imagination.

Nappies—We've come a long way from the scratchy towelling squares we used to fold into triangles and, somehow, pinned to fit our babies. Modern cloth nappies are beautifully designed to grow with babies—using different fasteners—and many come with a detachable absorbent pad and liner and plenty of online help on their use. Some can be used with biodegradable, disposable liners too. The bottom line (pardon the pun): you have to wash them.

There are also biodegradable nappies on the market. Another option is known as toileting or elimination communication, which is, basically, picking up the early signs that your child needs to go and rushing them onto the potty, leading to early toilet-training.

Verdict   Great colours, innovative fabrics and increasing choice in reusable nappies makes a big difference. If you stick to reusable nappies you'll halve your costs compared to disposables, according to Sustainability Victoria. One new mum we talked to who has done the sums was expecting to save even more; about $2500 over two years, based on 6000 nappies from birth to toilet training. She did say 'it's definitely more work' (but also 'I can't put that much waste into landfill'). Cloth nappies also come out ahead environmentally, even when washing[5] is taken into account.

Some parents say reusables aren't quite as good at keeping babies and clothes fresh and dry. A popular compromise is to use reusables at home and disposables when going out. And, while biodegradable nappies sound good, they are not flushable and so likely end up in landfill, just like regular disposables.

SEARCH TERMS   Q modern cloth nappies   Q nappy alternatives Q cloth diapers   Q toileting.

Wet wipes—What did we ever do without them? Well, not that long ago, our mums used washable cloths, like damp face washers, carried in a reusable wet bag to clean us up. One cloth for our faces, a different one for the other end. In a big mess emergency these cotton cloths could even be safely thrown away. By contrast wet wipes are a combination of synthetic fibres and cellulose. They shouldn't be flushed—but wreak havoc in our drains anyway—and should only be disposed of in landfill. Fortunately, lots of good-looking reusable washcloths are back on the market (in stores and online)—or make your own out of old towels. More expensive disposable 'natural' wipes are also available, mostly in plastic dispensers. Some can theoretically be flushed or composted—but check the packet.

Verdict Unless you are away from running water, reusable cloths are a viable alternative to wet wipes and, over the long term, they're cheaper. Washing isn't too difficult—you just need a bucket, a pair of latex laundry gloves, a washing machine and the sun to dry them.

SEARCH TERMS Q reusable baby wipes Q eco baby wipes
Q alternatives to baby wipes Q cloth baby wipes.

Feeding

Milk—Even if you are breastfeeding you'll probably need bottles as a back-up. Invest in BPA-free plastic and silicon teats, or glass bottles with silicon teats. Glass is ideal from a hygiene point of view, but some people are understandably reluctant to use a bottle that could break.

Solids—If you cook up baby food yourself, or mash fresh fruit, you won't be throwing away plastic packaging. This is not, of course, always practical. When buying ready-made, choose glass jars that can be recycled over squeezy pouches.

Pouches are rapidly increasing their share of the global baby food market, but as they are made of foil and plastic fused together they can't be recycled. Billions upon billions are going to landfill.[6] And while they are handy—they don't need refrigeration, can be thrown in a bag and reduce spills—they are also attracting the attention of developmental specialists. Concerns[7] have been raised that sucking food down denies young children the essential learning experiences of mastering spoons and forks, and the portable nature of the pouches erodes opportunities to establish regular, sit-down meal times. And as they are so easy to eat quickly they may lead to weight gain. These issues are interesting examples of how a material can change our lifestyle.

If you do need convenience, lots of companies are now making refillable pouches out of food-grade silicone that you can fill with food you've prepared yourself. Great if you are travelling or need to feed in the car or out and about—they can also be prepared in advance and frozen.

Similarly, silicone moulds can be used to make ice blocks that help with teething.

Snacks and drinks—It's very easy to get by without individually packaged kids' snacks and drinks. If you avoid them, your kid's diet will be healthier, too. Use small, coloured snack boxes and put interesting nibbles in them yourself. If you don't have time to cook, some snacks are available without plastic packaging at bulk stores. Kids don't need poppers with plastic straws either. Fill their own reusable drink bottle with water or watered-down juice—it's just as easy to squeeze an orange or two as it is to buy juice in plastic. Given the health issues linked to sugary drinks, this is a win–win.

Verdict Babies and toddlers need special attention. But once kids no longer need specially prepared food, refer to the tips in Chapter 5, The Kitchen.

SEARCH TERMS Q BPA-free baby bottles Q reusable food pouches Q reusable food sachets Q plastic-free baby.

Playing without plastic

The world is full of plastic toys and lots of them, like Lego, are made from plastics that have been tested as safe, even if your kids chew on them. You can avoid plastics altogether by choosing wooden toys, natural rubber and other lovely things like cloth books. Or, in the case of Lego, you can wait for the petroleum-based, plastic-free ethos unveiled in 2015 to work its way through the range. The Danish company has invested US$155 million in research to ensure Lego is made from fully sustainable materials by 2030.[8] The first blocks are on sale: 25 different types of Lego trees and plants made from sugar cane–derived bioplastics.

The biggest challenge posed by plastic toys, though, is excess. Cheap plastic means cheap toys and we've bought way too many of them. And as children grow out of toys quickly, our household waste collections are full of perfectly good toys from trinkets right up to outdoor plastic cubby houses, slides and trampolines. A US academic study published in 2017[9] concluded that too many toys reduces the quality of toddlers' play and having fewer toys actually helps young children focus and play creatively. So, less can be more!

By buying fewer toys and enjoying more experiences—like making cubby houses from cardboard boxes, for example, or going to the zoo—you can easily reduce your plastic footprint. You can also prevent plastic toys from entering the waste stream by making sure you pass them on to someone who can use them as your kids grow up. Spend a little time looking at your local buy, swap, sell websites to find out what you can give away, sell or pick up yourself.

But what if your kids are given most of their plastic toys as presents? That's up to you, but my personal opinion is to appreciate a gift, no matter what it is.

Verdict Online networks mean never having to dispose of plastic toys in landfill—pass them on and look for something different. Young kids don't notice if something is second-hand. For older kids, try providing experiences instead of more plastic stuff. Outings and online games and tokens for virtual worlds provide opportunities to treat kids without generating more demand for cheap plastics.

SEARCH TERMS Q BPA-free toys Q plastic-free toys Q natural rubber toys Q wooden toys Q toy library Q toy swap.

Clothes—See Chapter 8, Your Wardrobe. The good news in the baby and kids' clothes market is the arrival of more eco-friendly fabrics like bamboo, wool and organic cotton. Petroleum-derived synthetic fabrics are not always great against very young skin.

The Plastic-free Lunchbox Project

It started with a pile of colourful fabric scraps, an energetic mum, a committed teacher, and a great idea.

Together they taught kids at one Tasmanian primary school how to make their own beeswax wraps, the first step towards a plastic-free lunch box. The results were immediate. At Taroona Primary School in Hobart, where the first workshops were run, playground plastic litter has dropped significantly. The reason was clear: the single biggest source of plastic waste had been the cling film and zip-lock bags used to wrap sandwiches and other lunch items.

Now every one of the 350 or so kids at the school has their own beeswax wrap. And, because they made it themselves, out of fabric they chose, they have a sense of pride and ownership and are motivated to use it, says the project's founder, Sarah Bury.

The workshops have now reached ten Tasmanian schools, with many more scheduled. The formula is simple and easy to replicate. Children learn about plastics in the environment, then they select a pre-cut cotton square that they coat with beeswax. They also learn how to look after their wrap so it lasts, a starting point for conversations about waste solutions.

'It's nice to see how proud kids feel about their own wrap. Painting the wax onto the fabric is an easy, satisfying process that lets them know they can be part of the solution,' says Sarah.

The Hobart lawyer and mother of two young children says she was spurred into action by ABC TV's *War on Waste* in 2017. Her quest to understand more led her to the film *A Plastic Ocean* and a new awareness of the plastic litter around her local school, situated in a suburb fronting the Derwent River.

'I felt I couldn't just sit back and do nothing—so I started at the grassroots community level with the very modest expectation that if I could stop even one plastic bag going into the ocean that was better than nothing,' she says.

Her first step was to start Plasticwise Taroona, a small local group that's linked to a national network of about 50 similar groups across Australia, all working to reduce plastic waste within their communities. As it turns out, the group's cumulative impact has far exceeded even their most optimistic goals.

Prior to launching the plastic-free lunch box project, the Plasticwise Taroona volunteers used second-hand fabrics to sew about 1500 reusable shopping bags which they gave out at grocery stores across Tasmania, leading to the removal of plastic bags from the check-outs of a major chain. About 685,000 plastic bags have been avoided to date. And Sarah has also dramatically reduced her own family's plastic footprint.

With so many individually packaged snacks aimed at kids, including many sold as organic, is that difficult?

'It's just about keeping food simple. Kids don't need processed snacks even if they are sold as health foods— like fancy overpackaged yoghurt squeezy packs that can't be recycled,' she says.

And, with less plastic in their lives, the family has embraced a new culture.

'Even though I am probably even busier, with a job and the lunch-box project, I don't feel like giving up [throw-away] plastics has slowed us down. We eat more simply, we compost, we shop locally, we buy more carefully—and we don't buy lots of plastic toys. It's very nice going local!'

STANDING OUT IN THE PLAYGROUND– ONE MUM'S SOLUTION

It's hard enough when your kids are teased at school, but what if it's something you're doing that is singling them out?

Take Rachel's two young boys, who initially attracted unwanted attention in the playground for their plastic-free lunches in homemade beeswax wraps. Unsurprisingly, all they wanted was plastic packets of snacks and sandwiches wrapped in plenty of cling film.

Instead of relenting, Rachel Potter, a professional chef from Sydney's north, came up with a creative solution.

She invited groups of kids over after school to learn how to make their own simple crackers, with beetroot powder to colour them pink or charcoal powder to turn them black. The kids took the recipes home and got their parents interested.

Then she tackled easy cakes, teaching visiting kids how to whip up their own cake mix by combining a few simple, cheap ingredients and storing them in a jar, with instructions for cooking and customising their creation when they got home.

'I am naturally shy—so I don't say you shouldn't be buying packaged cake mix,' she says of her personal quest to reduce plastic use.

'Instead, I say here's a great cake mix that only costs 40 cents to make, your kids will love it.

'And, look, they have done it themselves!'

Rachel understands what it feels like to stand out at school. Raised by her grandmother, who got by on the aged pension, everything she had was homemade, including her school uniform. But money was so tight that while everyone else had four buttons, Rachel's grandmother could only stretch to two.

'If we couldn't grow it or make it, we didn't have it,' she says.

This waste not, want not upbringing is something she's now incredibly grateful for. It gave her the skills to turn the family's own urban plot into a productive kitchen garden, where they keep chickens and bees as well. It also meant she learned how to cook just about anything from scratch, even before she trained as a chef.

'As my children got older I knew I wanted to instil in them what it was to be more self-reliant, less dependent on food and other industries,' she says of her boys, now six and seven years old.

That includes reducing plastic. Big gains can be made, she says, by avoiding processed, overpackaged food by sourcing ingredients from the garden, markets and bulk stores and then cooking for yourself. Rachel also runs workshops to help people reduce food waste at Sydney's Cornersmith Cafe and Picklery.

Recently, she noticed a welcome shift. With more and more people interested in waste, other parents have been striking up conversations with her at school.

At home, her greatest satisfaction is her own boys' growing awareness. When the family ran out of honey for their toast one morning, instead of suggesting they go to the shops, her eldest son announced: 'Mum, you'll have to put your [protective] suit on and get some more from the beehive.'

'His instinct was to get it from the garden, not the supermarket—that spurred me on!'

Rachel's easy crackers

2 cups plain flour
¾ cup water
½ cup neutral oil (like rice bran or grapeseed)
about 2 teaspoons salt (or less to taste)
herbs and spices as desired

toppings as desired e.g. sesame seeds, nigella seeds, fennel seeds

(I add to my mix: 2 teaspoons each of ground fennel, onion powder and garlic powder. I also add some sort of colouring, e.g. ¾ teaspoon charcoal powder or 2 teaspoons beetroot powder.)

1. Preheat the oven to 170°C. Line four baking trays with compostable baking paper.
2. Combine all the ingredients in a bowl until they come together to form a dough.
3. Divide the dough between the baking trays and cover with another sheet of baking paper. Roll out the dough between the sheets of paper until about 2 mm thick.
4. Cut the rolled dough into the desired shapes.
5. Spray the dough very lightly with water and gently dust on your toppings.
6. Place the trays in the oven, in batches, if needed, and bake the crackers for 5 minutes. Switch the position of the trays in the oven and bake for another 5–10 minutes until the crackers are firm.
7. Transfer the crackers to a wire rack immediately to cool.

The crackers will keep for up to two weeks in an air-tight container at room temperature. You can make half this recipe if you have a small oven.

Thanks to Rachel Potter: www.cambridgehillfarm.com.au

How to throw a birthday party that's not rubbish

My sister Prema wanted a plastic-free party for her son, Kai, whose birthday happens to fall in July. She considered spruiking Plastic Free July on the invitations but decided not to, which was probably a good call. Have you heard of virtue signalling? I hadn't until recently. (I honestly thought people used KeepCups because they care, not to look virtuous in the coffee queue!) I also know that parenting can be a minefield. So you need to be careful not to imply you're criticising other people by trumpeting your own approach. So, no virtue signalling on the invitations. If you want to do a plastic-free or a plastic-lite party, well, just do it.

Decorations—Avoid balloons—they hurt wildlife. Try old-fashioned bunting made from paper and raffia, string or fabric—easy to make at home, or can be purchased, and can be re-used. Don't buy the bunting packs made of plastic! You could also go for colourful paper pom poms on string and paper streamers. And small vases of fresh flowers look great.

Serving platters—If you don't own enough yourself, borrow. Avoid single-use plastic and foil trays, designed to be used once and tossed.

Crockery, cutlery, serviettes etc.—For kids, glass isn't an option, so look for compostable paper cups, plates and bamboo cutlery or similar. You can find compostables online and in plenty of stores. If you go for paper-based products, they can be composted at home—but check labels, as bioplastics need a commercial composter. We use cotton tablecloths but big sheets of butchers' paper are also great, and kids can draw on them too.

Food—Here are a few ideas from Kai's party that went down well:

The cake—With no Disney-themed plastic tablecloth, cups and plates, we moved the theme to the cake. We ordered a butter cake with white icing and a *Cars* motif, then added two real toy cars, that doubled as gifts, for decoration.

Fairy bread—Buy sliced soft bread from the baker in paper bags. Use butter (paper-wrapped). Hundreds and thousands usually come in plastic but recycle the container or keep it to refill with herbs later.

Chocolate crackles—Using ingredients sourced from a bulk food store, combine melted cooking chocolate with puffed rice and desiccated coconut, then spoon into paper cases. Not the traditional recipe on the side of the Rice Bubbles box, but they taste great. Exact amounts can be purchased, so you have no leftover ingredients in the cupboard.

Filled bread rolls—Order ahead and ask the baker to put them straight into a cardboard box—we lined ours with clean tea towels. Put fillings out so people can help themselves. We used home-prepared pulled pork and coleslaw—all ingredients were easy to source plastic-free using our own containers.

Homemade sausage rolls—Easy to make at home, but some plastic is unavoidable if you use commercially prepared puff pastry. Fill the pastry with mince mixed with herbs, spices, onion, garlic and grated veggies.

Drinks—Offer flavoured water in jugs or drink dispensers using fruit slices of different colours.

Fruit—Set out colourful platters of fruit, including watermelon cut to look like trees.

Party bags—Use small paper bags, line with coloured serviettes and drop in unwrapped chocolates and sweets. Items like honeycomb squares and chocolate buttons can be purchased from bulk food stores, supermarkets have scoop and weigh ranges (they offer plastic bags for these—but put them in the paper bags used for mushrooms and place the price sticker on that). Otherwise, innovate! Smarties still come in cardboard boxes.

Clean up—All food scraps and crockery and cutlery were composted in an at-home bin. To speed up the break-down of paper plates and cups, soak them in water for a couple of days, then tear them into small pieces.

Verdict   We were left with one small reusable plastic shaker (from the hundreds and thousands) and a small handful of soft plastic (recycled at a supermarket).

SEARCH TERMS   Q scoop and weigh   Q bulk stores   Q eco party Q eco catering   Q bamboo catering.

CHAPTER 10

ENTERTAINING, AND EATING (AND DRINKING) OUT

Eek! The more I talk about going plastic-free, the more I notice all the plastics I still need to free myself from. That makes me acutely aware of my own behaviour. Never more so, perhaps, than when I've invited people over. I worry about falling short (although I do know we overestimate people's interest in us). I also worry that the legacy plastics in my apartment might give the wrong impression. By legacy plastics, I mean the many empties I haven't thrown out because they might come in handy for refills. So, what do you do if you want to host a plastic-free or plastic-lite dinner or drinks party? This question immediately exposes one of my greatest weaknesses—and personal plastic-free challenges—cheese and crackers and/or chips with a glass of wine. Here are some ideas. Remember: whatever you do is useful, you don't have to do everything at once.

Entertaining

The Nibbles Platter

Cheese—It's usually pre-cut and pre-packaged in plastic, but it doesn't have to be. Try going to the deli section of your supermarket or other food store and asking if they will cut you a piece off a cheese wheel and wrap it in paper. Soft cheeses, such as mozzarella and ricotta, can be fished out of the brine or cut off a bulk supply. You can bring in your own baking paper or your own container. But if you are going through the self-serve check-out at a supermarket your container will confuse the scales, so go via a staffed check-out and explain what you are doing to a real person.

I've also been able to buy whole small wheels of cheese in a supermarket just by going up to the information counter and asking—cheese lasts for ages and can be stored in the fridge in beeswax wraps or washable silicone wraps. (If hard cheese goes mouldy, it's still safe to eat once you've cut the mould off[1]). Bulk hard cheeses, like cheddar and parmesan, can also be grated in advance and stored in a container in the freezer—much cheaper than paying for packaging and processing.

Crackers—When you are avoiding plastic packaging it can seem like you will never bite into a crisp cracker again. Fortunately, this is not true. If you have a bulk store nearby, they stock crackers and snacks. Otherwise, buy a couple of baguettes from a local baker or supermarket; they are easy to find without plastic and come in white and various grain and flour types. Thinly slice them, then crisp them up in a warm oven—instant crackers! Or to make your own crackers, see the recipe in the previous chapter.

Chips—I love chips! You could make your own by thinly slicing potatoes or sweet potatoes, spraying with olive oil and baking in a hot oven. Timewise, this is quite a leap from rummaging in the pantry, pulling open a packet and dumping its contents in a bowl when friends drop in. You can't get potato chips at bulk stores, but you can get sweet potato chips, veggie chips and pretzels and other crunchy stuff made of things like chickpeas. Store them in airtight containers and no one will starve.

Dips—When I first realised how easy it could be to make dips I was a bit embarrassed about all those plastic tubs I'd bought over the years, and even more so about all the half-empty ones I'd left to go off in the back of the fridge. Hummus has three key ingredients that can be kept in the pantry—chickpeas, olive oil and tahini (in a glass jar). You can use canned chickpeas or soak fresh ones, then cook them in lots of boiling water (very cheap and easy). Blend a 400 gram can of chickpeas or 1½ cups of cooked chickpeas together with ¼ cup of tahini and 1½ tablespoons of extra virgin olive oil, plus a few good squeezes of lemon, a garlic clove and salt to taste, and it's done. Make it while your baguette slices are crisping in the oven. Once you've mastered this one, venture further afield.

Accompaniments—Things like chutneys, quince paste and olives come in jars, or add the real thing—slices of apple or pear and grapes, figs and dates all go well and can be found plastic-free.

The Main

If you plan your meals ahead and cook from scratch, you can avoid a lot of plastic packaging. It doesn't have to be fancy—keep it simple. Source your meat or fish from your local butcher or fishmonger and ask for it to be put straight into your own container. Fruit and veg are increasingly easy to find naked, oils come in glass bottles or metal cans, pasta can be found in cardboard packaging, rice can be bought in paper bags at bulk stores, and dried herbs and spices can be found at bulk stores and scooped out of large jars into small paper bags or your own containers. And, unless you live in an apartment without windows, you can grow fresh herbs in your garden or in pots on a balcony or windowsill.

An easy main to fall back on is marinated chicken and warm broccoli salad with crunchy bread; all ingredients can be found plastic-free.

Dessert

Many desserts can be plastic-free, especially if you make them yourself. Flour, eggs and sugar are all available in paper packaging. My go-to dessert is a chocolate chip cookie dough pot, pretty much a cookie baked in a ramekin. It's easy, delicious and makes you look like a dessert pro. To make, pick your favourite chocolate chip cookies recipe but replace the plastic-packaged choc chips with chocolate bars that come wrapped in paper and foil. Once the dough is made, spoon the mixture into ramekins (filling halfway up) and bake for about ten minutes or until golden, but not solid. Fruit is also really versatile—and plastic-free. In summer make a fruit platter; in winter bake a fruit crumble. The harder part is what you serve with dessert. Berries are almost impossible to source without a plastic punnet—unless you go to a berry farm and pick your own! Ice cream comes in containers that are plastic-lined, and yoghurt and cream are commonly sold in plastic tubs.

Try using cream that comes in small recyclable cartons. There are some easy ways to make ice cream at home—just search for no-churn or nice cream recipes.

Drinks

Most alcoholic beverages come in glass bottles or cans, and with container deposit schemes in some states we can be increasingly confident they will be recycled. But about half of us consume soft drinks and over a quarter of us buy bottled water every single week. As the host, you don't have to lug bags of PET bottles home just to be polite. Use a glass drink dispenser full of tap water (filtered, if you like) with something nice in it like lemon slices and mint or fruit. If you need fizzy water, invest in a SodaStream or similar so you can carbonate tap water at home in reusable bottles. You can mix your home sparkling water with freshly squeezed fruit juice to create another non-alcoholic option.

Crockery, cutlery, napkins etc.—See A Partyware Solution, below. My personal choice is to borrow if you don't have enough glasses and crockery yourself or look for pre-loved; charity stores are always well supplied with reasonable quality crockery and cutlery that costs next to nothing. Alternatively, look for compostable options.

Verdict With a bit of forward planning, entertaining at home doesn't have to generate huge garbage bags full of rubbish.

SEARCH TERMS   ⌕ zero-waste entertaining ⌕ plastic-free entertaining ⌕ eco party ⌕ wasteless pantry.

A PARTYWARE SOLUTION

When Tasmanian lawyer and mum Sarah Bury was talking to her younger brother about his upcoming birthday party, she realised he was planning to buy lots of plastic cups and other partyware. She had a better idea. What if she bought a set of glasses, cups, plates, platters and cutlery that anyone in the community could borrow when they entertained? Imagine how many disposable items they could avoid. Today, the set is available via Facebook to friends and family within reach of her home in Taroona, Hobart. 'All they have to do is message me with what they need and I put it on the doorstep,' she says. https://plasticwise.net/

The great Aussie sausage sizzle— without the trash

What about a barbecue? We've tested this en masse when we've been raising funds for a local community group over recent years. Here's what we did.

The brief—To cook about 600 sausages and piles of sliced onions, serve them on bread and offer tomato or barbecue sauce, plus drinks.

The challenge—A previous fundraiser generated lots of non-recyclable waste. We had counted 42 plastic or Styrofoam meat trays with wet, dirty cling wrap, about 50 plastic bread bags, 25–50 frozen onion bags (depending on size), two garbage bins full of empty drink cans and bottles, nine empty plastic sauce bottles and loads of food and paper serviette waste—all mixed in together!

So, we set ourselves the challenge of de-rubbishing the event. Cost is a big factor for fundraisers—so we had to match budget supermarket prices dollar for dollar. Here's how we went.

Sausages—We were looking for an alternative to pre-packaged trays of budget supermarket sausages. Googling didn't help, so we began by talking to our local butcher. We couldn't afford to buy his gourmet snags, so he referred us to a bulk meat supplier a couple of suburbs away. We rang and discussed what we were doing, and they were helpful. We ordered over the phone and arranged to pick the sausages up early on the day of the event in our own large reusable (food-grade) plastic containers—they happily put them straight in, without any packaging. (We kept them in eskies, so we needed to buy a few ice bags as a health and safety requirement.) Our bulk buy turned out to be cheaper than supermarket budget snags.

Onions—Frozen and pre-chopped onions are easy to buy. But if you have a food processor with the right attachment, or can borrow one, chopping or slicing is quick and easy. Slicing onions yourself saves about 25 per cent of the cost of frozen—and they taste better, too.

Oil—Buy in glass bottles or metal cans.

Bread—Talk to bakeries in the area and find one interested in your goal. What about using bread rolls? One roll does cost more than two slices of supermarket bread, but they are easier to serve and can be bought plastic-free. If you do go with rolls, arrange to pick them up in clean cardboard boxes lined with old tablecloths, and use the excess fabric to fold over the top to close. Sliced bread is more challenging, but some bakers will sell sliced loaves in paper bags, if you ask. More expensive or cost neutral.

Sauces—We bought the largest possible containers and decanted them into small, reusable squeeze bottles. Not an ideal solution, but we did save money and reduce waste. You could make sauces yourself, but this is very time consuming and expensive.

Drinks—We decided not to sell any soft drinks or bottled water and explained our reasoning to all our customers. Instead we used glass drink dispensers filled with filtered tap water and flavoured with sliced fruit and mint leaves. A couple more bags of ice were needed here. We charged 50 cents to cover the cost of each compostable paper cup; this included a little extra for a profit. There were no complaints!

Serviettes—We used unbleached, recycled paper.

Verdict A handful of plastic ice bags went to landfill, a couple of plastic sauce containers were sent to recycling, and all food and paper waste was composted. Not 100 per cent plastic-free, but pretty close—and 600 people got lunch!

SEARCH TERMS Q bulk meat supplies Q wholesale meat Q beverage dispensers Q drink dispensers Q compostable drink cups Q unbleached serviettes.

Eating (and drinking) out

Restaurants and cafes

Instead of getting take-away, think about sitting down and relaxing instead. Avoiding plastic packaging is a great excuse to enjoy a meal in a restaurant or cafe.

If you like food courts with lots of quick and easy meals on offer, check if they offer ceramic bowls and plates and real cutlery—some do. My sister ordered a Vietnamese pho for lunch recently and was handed a large plastic bowl with a lid containing the noodles and dry ingredients, another plastic cup with a lid with the hot stock, a plastic spoon and plastic chopsticks, a napkin and tiny plastic spice sachets— all of which were then packed in a single-use plastic bag. It is becoming easier to find food outlets that don't expect you to sit down and eat using disposable plastic plates, bowls and utensils. If you expect to have leftovers, bring a reusable container with you for the doggy bag.

Verdict Eating out is easy and shouldn't come with plastic! Even in food courts, just ask before you pay; you may be able to request bowls, cutlery and a real glass or cup. If not, look for another option!

SEARCH TERMS Q just type in your favourite food type and location and go from there!

WHERE ARE AUSTRALIA'S MOST RESPONSIBLE CAFES?

For Rachel Draper it's not just about the coffee, although that does matter. It's about what it comes in.

As the operations manager of Responsible Cafes, Rachel has spent countless volunteer hours thinking about how to reduce our collective plastic footprint, starting with our morning coffee fix. The answer she and her colleagues came up with was to offer customers a financial incentive to bring their own cup. To date, their network of more than 4200 cafes Australia-wide has avoided the use of some 51 million disposable cups that would otherwise end up in landfill. The goal is 100 million by the end of the year.

It works like this. Responsible Cafes links registered cafes on a searchable online map that directs coffee drinkers to participating businesses in their area. Cafes qualify for the listing by offering at least a 20-cent discount per cup of coffee, or another incentive, for a customer bringing their own reusable cup. Rachel says 70 per cent of registered cafes are offering at least 50 cents off per cup, with some offering up to $1 off.

The initiative goes back to Rachel's own early efforts to tackle plastics by taking part in beach and shoreline clean-ups. The 30-year-old consumer researcher says this seemingly endless task made her realise waste had to be tackled at the source.

When she first started using a reusable cup herself her local cafe was hesitant to accept it. Nowadays, she loves seeing people proudly carrying their reusable cups, a change she attributes partly to ABC TV's *War on Waste* as well as the growing number of social media campaigns.

But it's not just about changing cafe culture. Coffee is a gateway to much more.

'We've found that once people change one behaviour, they are open to looking at other things—it's a change in mindset,' she says.

'So, once they've started thinking about their coffee cup, they think about other things like plastic bags, straws and water bottles.'

What's also shifting are the images on our screens that we subliminally file away as normal behaviour; every photo or video post, or new TV series or movie, showing take-away coffee in reusable cups helps. So does getting out on the street and talking.

When Responsible Cafes took a closer look at their membership data in 2018 they discovered some interesting trends. Inner-city Brisbane was leading the push away from disposable cups, ahead of Sydney city, with Melbourne city third despite its status as Australia's self-appointed coffee capital.

The data reflected areas where local councils have strong sustainability programs and where active local influencers live. Ryde, in suburban north-western Sydney, was fourth, followed by Wollongong city, the Sunshine Coast region in Queensland, Geelong, Adelaide city, Yarra city and Queensland's Gold Coast. Which shows what you do locally really does matter.

With at least 25 new cafes a week joining up, Rachel is incredibly busy just keeping up her day job and her voluntary role. She's not an antiplastic evangelist, just someone who does as much as she can, she says. Which turns out to be a pretty long list, including shopping at bulk stores, swapping clothes with friends, carrying reusable cutlery, a straw and a water bottle, and making her own beauty and cleaning products.

'But I don't beat myself up if I occasionally have a chocolate bar—if everyone did a few things, it would make a huge difference.'

Drinking out

Just say no to plastic straws and start up conversations about why you're avoiding them. Or whip out your personal, reusable straw made of bamboo or shiny metal that you keep in its own cloth sleeve! There are plenty of venues to pick from that have signed up with groups like Sydney Doesn't Suck, The Last Straw and Straw No More!

Verdict You can do this! You might consider this as a good place to start your quitting-plastic journey—you can practise your plastic-free spiel on the bartender when you ask for 'no straw'.

SEARCH TERMS 🔍 reusable straws 🔍 plastic-straw free 🔍 straw-free venues.

Take-away

What if you could eat the containers your food and drinks come in? Would that help? Think of an ice-cream cone. Personally, it's my favourite plastic-free snack, especially at the beach. Even if it's dropped on the sand, it won't cause any long-term grief. What about kebabs rolled up in flatbread, and other kinds of wraps? No plastic needed, just a serviette to hold them with. In many cultures flatbreads made of wheat or maize have been used to wrap food or are torn up and used to scoop or mop it up, no need for cutlery. Likewise, there are all sorts of natural wrappings, like palm and banana leaves, that are coming back via new biopackaging options. There are also new ranges of compostable packaging made from bagasse, the waste left over after sugar cane is processed, and cutlery made from plant starch.

No-waste edible containers and cutlery might seem far-fetched, and I am sceptical about edible coffee cups that are supposed to hold hot liquid for up to 40 minutes. I think the so-called 'Scoff-ee Cup',[2] for example, that's made from biscuits, lined with white chocolate and wrapped in branded (KFC) sugar paper, looks more like a publicity stunt for the global fast-food chain than an environmental initiative. But I am very interested in a new range of bowls and cutlery designed 'not to last'.[3] They're made in India by Afghan refugees from flour pastes of various grains— harking back to the traditional use of breads to hold food. I don't know what they taste like, but they are easy to compost even if they aren't delicious. Carrying a reusable cutlery kit is another way of avoiding plastic cutlery (see Chapter 11, The End of Single-use Plastic?). There's also lots to be optimistic about when you consider the advances in biopackaging. Bioplastics, made from crops like corn or agricultural waste, make up only one per cent of the global plastics market right now, but interest and sales are exploding. However, as biopackaging is currently more expensive than many cheap plastics, you might want to vote with your wallet and encourage a switch.

Another option is to BYO. A friend of mine recently had a casual lunch meeting with a client from a sustainability company. When arranging their meeting, the client offered to bring a plate along for my friend, as they were grabbing lunch to go. My local Thai take-away allows me to bring my own old plastic containers from home when I'm getting take-away and puts my order straight into them when it's ready.

Verdict This biggest challenge is probably in our heads. It is okay to bring your own containers to pick up take-away food, but you need to be willing to challenge the status quo and to start a conversation with your favourite local food outlets. You also need to be willing to forgo the convenience of delivery! With edible options like ice-cream cones, just go for it!

SEARCH TERMS
Q reusable food containers Q portable cutlery sets Q folding cutlery Q bento boxes Q tiffin containers.

Vote with your wallet

Give your business to a cafe that will wrap your sandwich in paper and put it in a paper bag, no cling film involved. Buy a hamburger and chips that come in a cardboard or bio-box made from sugar cane, not in Styrofoam. Frequent a Thai take-away that's happy for you to bring your own containers and refuse the usual pile of single-use plastic containers. And make sure you get your food without a plastic bag. What about home-delivery services like Uber Eats and Deliveroo? There's no packaging information on their sites (well, not yet) but word of mouth can tip you off to which restaurants are using compostable packaging.

One issue to consider, though, is exactly what compostable means. Currently, much of the new generation of compostable bioplastics will only break down in hot industrial facilities—it's no good throwing them in a home compost bin. And our waste infrastructure is lagging behind, so many people don't yet have access to a collection that goes direct to industrial composters. That's something to pester councils and government about.

CHAPTER 11

THE END OF SINGLE-USE PLASTIC?

In Britain, the Iceland chain of supermarkets has a new plastic-free logo on their home-brand products that enables customers to choose their purchases based on how they are packaged. The rationale is simple: 'Our trust mark cuts through the confusion and tells you just one thing—this packaging is plastic-free and therefore guilt-free,' says Sian Sutherland of A Plastic Planet, the campaign behind the scheme.[1] In the Netherlands, consumers can already steer their supermarket trolleys down the world's first plastic-free aisles. And soon, when you take your shopping home, you might even be able to put them into a fridge lined with bioplastics made from sugar cane and corn. The plastic-free fridge prototype was revealed by Electrolux in 2018 (although how you might later compost a fridge is less clear).[2] Research by the international packaging industry found consumers in 2018 were most concerned about sustainability, ranking it ahead of convenience in second place. They also found some of us are willing to pay more for products in environmentally friendly packaging.[3]

Beyond the supermarkets, bulk food stores and waste-free businesses are springing up everywhere—from Sydney to Singapore to Stockholm. Their point of difference is also simple: good-quality food and products without the over-packaging. Online, interest in plastic-free shopping is just as keen. Even in the air, the plastic scourge is being tackled; at least one major international airline is discussing replacing all the plastic that currently arrives on your meal tray with compostable, plant-based alternatives. 'The supermarkets are the real litmus test,' says Paul Medeiros, founder of The Source Bulk Foods. 'Once supermarkets move, an issue has gone from a niche concern to the mainstream.' So, are we at the beginning of the end of single-use plastic?

The answer is a resounding 'yes', says Richard Fine, founder of the Australian-based sustainable packaging company BioPak, which introduced compostable bioplastics to a then-wary market over a decade ago. Over the past year, however, there's been a torrent of interest, he says.

'Consumers have a big role to play. Public awareness of plastic pollution has exploded and people are up in arms—and they are telling businesses they want something different.

'The push against plastics was originally a hippy fringe movement—now it is mainstream.'

A fork in the road

What will a plastic-lite future look like? Are we heading towards a post-disposable society? Will we all carry our own reusable coffee cups, cutlery, straws and water bottles, and eat in instead of driving through? Will we find we've outgrown retail therapy and the accumulation of stuff, and choose instead to spend our disposable income on experiences like live entertainment, travel and sport? Or will the demand for convenient consumption prevail? Could we continue to shop and toss unburdened, as a new generation of greener materials like compostable packaging and plant-based bioplastics replaces conventional plastics? We are now at a fork in the plastic-packaging road.

What's driving change is us. All those efforts around the world—small and large—to address plastic pollution and to refuse plastic packaging are sending powerful messages up the line that more and more people want to shop with the knowledge that they are not rubbishing the planet.

Governments everywhere are responding with aspirational targets and statements. The Australian Packaging Covenant commits businesses to a target of 100 per cent reusable, recyclable or compostable packaging by 2025.[4] New Zealand has banned single-use plastic bags. Internationally, policymakers are releasing numerous aspirational documents. The United Nations Environmental Program is encouraging us to end our 'toxic relationship' with plastic, by 'breaking up' with single-use plastics. The European Union has announced the first Europe-wide plastics strategy calling for all plastics to be recycled or reused and the banning or restriction of disposable single-use plastics like straws, take-away food containers, cotton buds and plastic drink stirrers. Across Asia and Africa bans on single-use plastic bags are in force or being rolled out in stages, including in China and India. A French ban on all petroleum-derived plastic plates and cutlery, the first in the world, is due to come into force in 2020.

We all know future targets can easily be missed, and some existing bans on single-use plastics are poorly enforced. But big businesses are lining up to announce their plans. For example, the global consumer goods giant, Unilever (think brands like Streets, Lipton, Bushells, Lux, Dove, Sunsilk and Continental, to name a few) has committed to 100 per cent reusable, recyclable or compostable packaging by 2025.[5] A 2018 editorial in the plastics industry magazine *Plastic News Europe* acknowledged that the tide has turned against fossil fuel–derived plastics. 'Public opinion has now turned downright cantankerous—backed up this time by all manner of plans and bans,'[6] it said, in a special edition devoted to one solution: a new generation of bioplastics.

What are bioplastics and compostables?

Most of us know that conventional plastics are made from the by-products of oil refining. But we're only just starting to realise we have a wealth of cheap, renewable natural resources around us that can be used for much the same thing. Bioplastics can be made from humble bacteria, algae, agricultural waste and even the yuck that abattoirs throw away. That means a clear drink cup marked with an enviro emblem might look and perform like conventional PET (used for soft-drink bottles) but it may be made from corn, sugar cane or cassava. On the commercial market these products are relatively new. But as novel as they currently seem, scientists have known about bioplastics since the mid-1800s. However, when the mass production of plastics took off in the 1950s, oil was cheap and abundant—and the environmental impact of plastic waste hadn't even been imagined. So there was little interest in the commercialisation of bioplastics.[7] Over the past twenty years that's all changed. A booming global bioplastics industry is expanding rapidly—albeit off a small base.

So, it's worth getting to know some new acronyms such as PLAs, PHAs and TPS. Polylactic acids (PLAs) were identified as early as 1845 but they were not commercially manufactured until the 1990s. They are produced using bacteria to ferment starch or sugars. We are already using the first generation of PLAs; these are mostly made from crops like corn. PHAs (polyhydroxyalkanoates) also use microorganisms for fermentation but can feed off pretty much any sugars or fats, or even the problematic greenhouse gas methane. Depending on what kind of bioplastic is needed, they can be produced from things like municipal waste, used vegetable oils, a wide range of plant waste, fatty acids and the methane that escapes from landfill sites. TPS (thermoplastic starches) use starches, so think about foods like potatoes and rice.

Turning full circle

I won't pretend to understand how to make bioplastics from plants and other naturally occurring things any more than I understand how to make plastics from oil. But I do know they're important. Ironically, the mass manufacture of petroleum-based plastics was, briefly, seen as a cheap solution to acute pressures on natural resources like wood and even ivory and tortoiseshell. The development of bioplastics derived from food and agricultural waste, or even bacteria, algae and chitin (from the exoskeletons of critters like crustaceans and insects, and the cell walls of fungi) would give us many of the benefits of conventional plastics without their environmental impacts. Can we have our cake and eat it? Maybe.

We're already using the first generation of bioplastics made from food crops like corn, rice, wheat and sugar cane. Waste-based bioplastics in the pipeline will address concerns that turning over agricultural land to packaging risks food security to the detriment of the world's poor. But there are still some barriers to their widespread use. Bioplastics are currently more expensive than petroleum-based plastics and there's still plenty of scientific and industrial development to do. The key limitation, however, is disposal. They are only valuable new wonder products if they find their way into the right compost streams. That means getting them to industrial composting facilities that keep them at around 60°C to decompose (the temperature of home compost bins is variable, and almost always cooler). A major 2018 report by the United Nations Environment Program concluded bioplastics and other natural alternatives to plastics show 'great potential'. But only if we design and build industrial composting facilities and collection systems to match—and if businesses and ordinary citizens make the effort to put them in the right bin.

That might seem obvious. But the global plastic pollution crisis is the result of two main human failings: we have not valued and recaptured plastics for recycling on any meaningful scale; and we've treated the natural environment like a rubbish tip. That model won't work for compostables either; as litter in the environment they'll still threaten ecosystems in much the same way as plastics, although they will break down faster.

Richard Fine says BioPak is working to demonstrate bioplastics are a feasible, practical and economically viable solution. He's encouraged by the construction of a new PLA plant in Thailand, using sugar-cane waste, and massive investments in new bioplastics in Europe. He believes businesses are reacting quickly to a consumer backlash against plastic pollution, and it will be big supermarkets and fast-food chains that will trigger a stampede away from products like plastic straws and single-use bags.

'I can see a future in which we manufacture products and packaging (from renewable materials) that have a positive environmental impact. I believe we are evolving to mimic nature (with plant-based packaging that is then composted).'

Fine previously worked in the petroleum-based plastics industry but was concerned about their impact. He is now optimistic about the potential for closing the materials loop. 'I can see a future in which consumers can use packaging without guilt,' he says, but that will require progress in waste management.

TONY SMALL—INNOCENT PACKAGING, NZ

Take a stroll through Auckland's CBD clutching a take-away coffee and, chances are, your used cup won't go to waste.

With so many Auckland cafes and food outlets now using coffee cups with plant-based liners—in place of plastic—a new network of bins has just been installed. Instead of going to landfill, these distinctive cardboard bins direct compostable coffee and drink cups, containers and wrappers—as well as leftover food—to industrial composting facilities. There they are turned back into soil conditioners, mimicking a natural life cycle.

This new closed-loop waste system is not a government initiative. The bins are provided by Innocent Packaging—a New Zealand supplier of plant-based, compostable packaging—and go to a private industrial composting facility. Is this the post-plastic model of the future?

'I know people are busy and that convenience is important. So, the idea is that you can still buy a coffee or food on the run—but without plastic,' says the Innocent Packaging Managing Director, Tony Small.

'Instead you get a plant-based disposable container—and once you've finished it's just as easy to find a bin for compostables on the street.'

Innocent Packaging sells a range of compostable food and drink containers for take-away businesses—some made from agricultural waste from wheat and sugar-cane processing. Others are more complex bioplastics that use corn, instead of fossil fuels, as a carbon source. But if they aren't composted and end up in landfill, they generate damaging methane gas, just like ordinary waste.

Tony is also well aware that simply replacing plastics with compostables may only be part of the solution. And why pander to lazy customers who could make the effort to bring their own reusable KeepCup or drink bottle?

It's a question he's asked himself many times. Prior to establishing Innocent Packaging, Tony sold a line of reusable coffee cups in 25 countries.

'We found the reusable cups went really well for the first six or eight weeks, but then usage fell off as people forgot to bring them or to wash them out—and went back to plastic-lined take-away cups.'

As a 33-year-old millennial, Tony says he's 'time poor and working hard in a fast-paced world', as are most of his peers. Personally, he doesn't want to have to carry reusable containers.

'My motivation was to simplify sustainability. I wanted it to be easy for myself and everyone else.'

Compostable containers and bioplastics are currently more expensive than fossil fuel–derived plastics, sometimes significantly so. Styrofoam (polystyrene), for example, is very cheap and holds food and liquids well, but it's so environmentally problematic it has been banned in places like New York City and across other US cities.

'Initially, we were mostly supplying stores that stocked organic products and free-range foods. But there's been a big change. Plastic is now talked about on a daily basis,' he says.

Businesses who don't heed this mood shift could damage their reputations and bottom line.

'I don't see how we can continue to do what we are doing and live in a world we are proud of.

'I have always believed we need to move away from single-use plastic, I just didn't realise how fast it could happen.'

A post-disposable society

By the mid-2020s could we be living in a post-disposable world?

The co-founder of KeepCup, Abigail Forsyth, thinks so. She's seen reusable coffee cups go mainstream, and she believes this is a more environmentally friendly solution than manufacturing disposable cups that are used only for minutes—even if they are plant-based.

But there's more to this than sustainability. There's also cultural and generational change underway. The US educational consultant Marc Prensky coined the term 'digital native', which refers to anyone who has had access to computers and connectivity their entire lives. So that encompasses pretty much anyone born from the 1980s in industrialised countries. What has this got to do with waste in general, and plastics in particular?

Online worlds and commerce have allowed us to have rich experiences and to accumulate virtual collections without having to own lots of stuff, in its physical form. We can also access music, videos and entertainment online. In short, we've shifted from a world in which everything—from letters to books and games—was acquired physically, to more transient experience-driven lives. At the same time, digital connectivity has enabled the rise of the share economy. We can forgo individual accumulation and opt into share systems for cars and bikes and we can buy, swap and sell pretty much anything else online, too. Think of all those used kids' toys, furniture, clothes, garden tools and equipment—in fact, anything you can imagine—that doesn't have to end up in landfill but can be picked up by a new owner.

'The next generation coming through has very little need for stuff, they are online—we will probably be regarded as the most wasteful and stuff-focused generation,' says Abigail.

'Nowadays, we can get a lot of what we want from our screen—information, education, entertainment—but when we venture out we also want to experience a pristine natural world.'

This could be a recipe for less rubbish. I'd like to think it is. But I also know I might sound starry-eyed and naive. My generation isn't exactly allergic to convenience. Think lying in bed, binge-watching a TV series, then summoning food via the Uber Eats app or similar and instructing the poor underpaid guy on the delivery bike to pass your food through the window, just to avoid the extra effort of making it to the front door. (I am not making this up, this is a true millennial flatmate story.)

The New Plastics Economy, the most comprehensive global report on single-use plastic packaging, projects plastic use will double again over the next twenty years and with it plastic pollution. Famously, it predicts more plastic waste in our oceans than fish by 2050.[8] Dismantling the convenience model of industrial plastics is a huge task. It's not just the restructuring of established industries, who will certainly object. It goes back to cultural change. That is, challenging our relationship to a material that has shaped the way we live.

'The real solution is an inconvenient one—making and using less plastic and promoting reusables,' says Stiv Wilson of the US-based The Story of Stuff Project,[9] which is true. The future, however, is ours to influence.

WHAT MORE CAN I DO?

I haven't yet seen 'STRAWkling' or 'plogging' on the list of new words to be added to the *Oxford Dictionary*, but if you want to do even more to combat plastic pollution, they might be useful terms to know. The 'STRAWkle' was invented at Sydney's Manly Cove, when the first group of young women went snorkelling to retrieve plastic straws from the shallow waters. Straws are hazardous to lots of sea creatures. In the case of Manly Cove, there's a precious remnant population of fairy penguins to protect, the last mainland breeding colony in New South Wales; there are local octopi (the somewhat ridiculous-sounding plural for octopus); lovely fragile-looking seahorses and much more. 'Plogging' is claimed by the Swedes, although lots of groups around the world have been doing it, just without such an enticing name. It's a blend of 'to jog' and 'to pick up' in Swedish—'plocka upp'. So, it just means running with a rubbish bag (and filling it up).

What everyone can do is 'pester'. You've seen how pester power works for brands who want kids to influence their parents' spending. It can also work against plastic. Do whatever you do best, email, call, blog, comment on social media—make a sign and jump up and down in the street. But do get in touch with supermarkets, councils, politicians and even your favourite brands. Tell them you'd be a much happier consumer if you didn't get so much plastic at the till. It does work. There are also lots of groups to join and activities to take part in that will connect you with other like-minded people. Some of our favourites are listed below, but try looking around your local area for more.

HOW TO HOST A STRAWKLE

Harriet Spark says she's all about the little changes. In her case, they've already added up to a movement that's original, interesting and growing—one (less) plastic straw at a time.

When the 26-year-old graphic designer and her friends decided to turn their passion for underwater worlds into a campaign to clean up plastic straws in the ocean, STRAWkling was born.

A year or so on, Harriet can be found every weekend at Manly Cove leading groups of up to 50 volunteers who are taking beach cleaning to the next level. Instead of merely picking through the sand and scouring the shoreline, they dive or snorkel offshore to remove hundreds of plastic straws from the water.

It can seem like a job that's never done. Manly, in Sydney's north, is a popular beach destination and home to hundreds of cafes, restaurants and take-away food outlets churning out mountains of waste, including plastic straws. And, every week, no matter how many were collected the previous weekend, there are just as many to collect.

But STRAWkling is not a futile effort, says Harriet.

Clean-ups are just the beginning. With a session or two of role-play training under their belt, the STRAWklers began engaging with Manly's cafes in early 2018. They wanted to show business owners just how many plastic straws were ending up in the water and to ask for their support. The results were a new group of businesses that are now 'Proudly Plastic Straw Free'.

One especially gratifying result came via social media. While the STRAWklers were swimming beneath Manly's ferry wharf, the owners of the two popular venues that sit directly over the water became interested in what was going on. So interested, in fact, that they decided to stop giving out plastic straws altogether. When they made their announcements on social media, they simply tagged Harriet and the STRAWklers.

'A large part of the solution to plastics pollution is awareness,' Harriet says. She didn't understand the threat of plastic herself until she trained as a diving instructor on the Great Barrier Reef after leaving school. That opened her eyes to plastics in the ocean, and triggered her own shift away from single-use plastics.

Her plastic-free life is still very much a work in progress, she says. She plans meals carefully to avoid waste and shops at local markets for package-free fresh produce. She also avoids the big four—take-away coffee cups, bottled water, plastic straws and single-use plastic bags—and washes her hair with a shampoo bar.

'I don't live entirely plastic-free because it is too hard—and I don't think consumers should have to feel guilty because of the way food is packaged for sale.'

On the other hand, she says, convenience shouldn't trump everything else.

'If I don't have my reusable coffee cup with me, I don't get a take-away coffee. We live in such a priv-ileged society—not getting one coffee is not going to kill you!'

Establishing STRAWkling has taken Harriet hun-dreds of volunteer hours. In summer, participants travel from across Sydney to join her, or even from other cities. On cold winter Sunday mornings, it's much harder to get out of bed early to go to the beach. But she does.

'Sometimes I get really overwhelmed and quite emotional,' she says, of seeing so much rubbish in the oceans around Australia, and around the world, through her face mask.

'But then it reminds me that I am trying to make a change—and that motivates me to keep going.'

Plastic Free July:
www.plasticfreejuly.org/about.html

You've probably heard of Dry July, so if you have tried going without alcohol for a month, then plastic shouldn't be too hard. Plastic Free July (PFJ) started as a small initiative in 2011, when a group of colleagues in Western Australia committed to reducing their plastic waste for a month. Today, more than three million people from 177 countries sign up to cut down or entirely eliminate their plastic consumption for the month of July. It's a great way to build your plastic-free habits; the website and online community offer tips to get started, problem-solving and support.

Take 3: www.take3.org

The idea behind Take 3 is simple—take three pieces of rubbish with you every time you leave the beach, a water way or, really, anywhere. It's an idea that, as it spreads, makes a bigger and bigger impact. The organisation was founded in 2009 in Australia in response to the growing problem of pollution in the marine environment. Now it's international, and runs school and community education programs. You can get involved by taking three pieces of rubbish out of the natural environment each time you go out, or join one of their larger local clean-up groups.

Two Hands project: www.twohandsproject.org

The Two Hands project aims to capture the spirit of national clean-up days on a local and regular basis. The basic idea is: take 30 minutes and two hands and clean up your world—anytime, anywhere. Two Hands also encourages participants to share photos of their haul on social media— not only demonstrating to a wider audience just how vast the scale of the plastic problem is, but also showing how easy it is to make a difference. Grab some gloves and some friends and collect waste for 30 minutes—then take a picture and share it via Facebook or info@twohandsprojct.org.

Responsible Runners: www.responsiblerunners.org

Before the Swedish fitness craze of plogging took off, there was Responsible Runners. If you like to combine your exercise with community service, this is the group for you. Responsible Runners meet at local beaches to run (or walk) along the coastline while picking up rubbish. In their first year, they picked up over 160,000 pieces of litter. They run in fifteen locations around Australia.

Responsible Cafes: responsiblecafes.org

Responsible Cafes connects coffee lovers and cafe owners who are making a conscious effort to reduce waste.

Australians throw away an estimated three billion take-away cups and lids every year—creating a long-lasting plastic legacy for a drink that often takes just ten minutes to finish. To encourage customers to use reusable coffee cups, Responsible Cafes offer a discount ranging from 20 cents to $1 to customers who bring their own. Find your nearest Responsible Cafe on their online cafe map.

The Last Straw: www.laststraw.com.au

The Last Straw is campaigning to reduce the use of plastic straws in venues all around Australia. You can support their efforts by ordering your next drink without a straw, or if you're involved with a venue, suggest that it becomes a member venue of The Last Straw—that is, a venue that doesn't offer plastic straws to their customers. You can also choose to spend your hard-earned cash in thoughtful venues that display a 'Proudly Plastic Straw Free' sticker.

Boomerang Bags: boomerangbags.org

Boomerang Bags is creating free reusable bags and getting them out into the community. Volunteers get together to make bags out of recycled materials and then give them away—free!—to their family, friends and even strangers in the supermarket check-out line so they'll have no excuse for accepting a single-use plastic bag. The movement began in Burleigh Heads, Queensland in 2013, but there are now hundreds of BB communities around the world, including 75 in New Zealand. Use their website to find a local BB group near you. Or, if there isn't one, start your own.

Dive Against Debris:
www.projectaware.org/diveagainstdebris/

Are you a diver? You could be part of Dive Against Debris, a citizen-science program that is pulling rubbish out of the oceans and, at the same time, collecting data to improve policies for waste management. Run by the international group Project Aware, the program has a survey kit and instructions about how to report your debris data online. If you want to take it to the next level, dive instructors and centres can adopt a local dive site and organise teams to protect it from plastic waste. Check their website for locations near you.

Clean Up Australia: www.cleanup.org.au

Clean Up Australia works with communities to 'clean up, fix up and conserve our environment'. On the first Sunday of March each year, it organises a national clean-up day. You can get involved by looking for a clean-up happening in your area, or if there isn't one, by nominating a site and starting your own clean-up crew. This is a great option if you want to do something but can't take on an ongoing commitment—it's just one day a year. It also provides a valuable insight into what's leaking into our environment; Clean Up Australia logs what's picked up, much of which is single-use plastic.

Plastic Free NZ:
osof.org/portfolio/plastic-free-nz/

Plastic Free NZ is a campaign run by Our Seas Our Future Charitable Trust that aims to make New Zealand, well, plastic free. They do this by raising awareness of the harmful effects of plastic on the environment and advocating for environmentally friendly solutions. Go to their website for the many way you can get involved in this campaign, like using their letter template to encourage businesses in your area to phase out plastic bags and straws, committing to Straw Free September, or joining a coastal clean-up near you.

Sustainable Coastlines: sustainablecoastlines.org

Sustainable Coastlines has a vision for New Zealand: Beautiful Beaches, Healthy Waters and Inspired People. This charitable trust coordinates large-scale coastal clean-ups, restores and plants riparian vegetation, and runs education programs. You can get involved by signing up for a training session or volunteering through their website.

Project Jonah: www.projectjonah.org.nz/ Get+Involved/Beach+Clean-ups.html

Project Jonah has been 'saving whales since 1974'. This registered charity is committed to protecting marine life by keeping plastic out of our oceans and waterways, as well as through marine mammal rescues. You can get involved by signing up for your local beach clean-up, removing plastic debris that harms marine mammals, or become a marine mammal rescuer.

ACKNOWLEDGEMENTS

Acknowledgements have always been one of my favourite parts of a book. Because, with any big undertaking, it is never just the people at the front that have made it happen, but also all the people that have held them up. On that note, I would like to thank everyone that spoke to us for the book. Thank you for sharing your stories, your tips and for the work you do. Thank you to my family for tolerating my early experiments with quitting plastic (and the pervasive smell of vinegar that came with them) and for embracing the plastic-free life, especially KP and Ellie (our illustrator). Thank you to my late grandmother, Margaret, for everything; you taught me how to stand up and be counted and I miss you very much. Thank you to my beautiful partner, Sophie, for all your support, including learning the Croatian word for straw so we could refuse them while on holiday. Most of all, thank you to my mum, Louise. This book was your idea (and mostly your writing) and I am so thankful to have been able to do it with you.

—*Clara Williams Roldan*

To every single person who has ever stopped to pick up rubbish on the street, on the beach or in the bush, or who has turned down a plastic bag or switched to a reusable coffee cup, thank you! Ditto to all those amazing groups in the community who devote their time to reducing plastic waste, whether they're out snorkelling for plastic straws in the ocean or sewing fabric bags and handing them out for free at the shops. You are the real heroes of this story! This book was a joy to research and write with my daughter Clara, because it gave us the opportunity to meet so many positive people (thanks for your time!) and to do something positive ourselves. That's a nice change—plastic pollution and its impacts can sometimes feel overwhelming. Thank you too to my wonderful family and friends who supported this project from the outset; my mum, Margaret, who passed away during the writing on this book, my husband, Craig, daughters Prema and Ellie (Elowyn), my cousin, Anna, and my coffee buddies Cathy, Rebecca, Jacky, Kelly, Mel and Martyn. And, as always, our cats, who kept my lap warm at the keyboard.

—*Louise Williams*

NOTES

CHAPTER 2: GOOD PLASTIC, BAD PLASTIC

1 V.E. Yarsley and E.G. Couzens, *Plastics*, Penguin Books Limited, Middlesex, 1945, p. 149.

2 Susan Freinkel, *Plastic: A toxic love story*, Text Publishing, Melbourne, 2011.

3 Karen Laird, 'Has PHA's time come?' in *Materials, Sustainability*, 3 August 2015, www.plasticstoday.com/materials/has-pha-s-time-come/90860424223038.

4 Richard C. Thompson, Shanna H. Swan, Charles J. Moore and Frederick S. vom Saal, 'Introduction: Our plastic age source', *Philosophical Transactions of the Royal Society B: Biological sciences*, The Royal Society Publishing, London, 2009, vol. 364, no. 1526.

5 A.L. Andrady and M.A. Neal, 'Applications and societal benefits of plastics', *Philosophical Transactions B*, 2009, vol. 364, no. 1526, pp. 1977–84.

6 www.triplepundit.com/2007/03/askpablo-glass-vs-pet-bottles/.

7 World Economic Forum, *The New Plastics Economy: Rethinking the future of plastics*, World Economic Forum and Ellen MacArthur Foundation, January 2016, p. 24, www3.weforum.org/docs/WEF_The_New_Plastics_Economy.pdf.

8 Vinny R. Sastri, *Plastics in Medical Devices: Properties, requirements, and applications*, William Andrew, 2013, p. 23.

9 Sastri, *Plastics in Medical Devices*, p. 23.

10   https://medlineplus.gov/ency/article/002975.htm.

11   www.cleanup.org.au/plastic bags.

12   www.newshub.co.nz/home/new-zealand/2018/03/new-push-for-plastic-bag-ban.html.

13   www.stuff.co.nz/world/103815176/plastic-bag-found-in-mariana-trench-deepest-place-on-earth.

14   Richard C. Thompson, Charles J. Moore, Frederick S. vom Saal and Shanna H. Swan, 'Plastics, the environment and human health', *Philosophical Transactions*, 2009, vol. 364, p. 2154.

15   Thompson, Moore, vom Saal and Swan, 'Plastics, the environment and human health', p. 2154.

16   Roland Geyer, Jenna Jambeck and Kara L. Law, 'Production, use and fate of all plastics ever made', *Science Advances*, 2017, vol. 3, no. 7.

17   www.abc.net.au/news/2016-01-21/microbeads-beauty-exfoliating-products-environmental-damage/7095108.

18   www.european-bioplastics.org/news-in-brief-march-2018.

19   www.theguardian.com/environment/2016/jun/20/microfibers-plastic-pollution-oceans-patagonia-synthetic-clothes-microbeads.

20   https://theconversation.com/ten-stealth-microplastics-to-avoid-if-you-want-to-save-the-oceans-90063.

21   http://science.sciencemag.org.wwwproxy1.library.unsw.edu.au/content/360/6384/28.full.

22   www.nzherald.co.nz/nz/news/article.cfm?c_id=1&objectid=11983980.

23   www.choice.com.au/food-and-drink/food-warnings-and-safety/plastic/articles/plastics-and-food.

24   www.choice.com.au/food-and-drink/food-warnings-and-safety/plastic/articles/plastics-and-food.

25   Thompson, Moore, vom Saal and Swan, 'Plastics, the environment and human health', p. 2164.

26   https://theconversation.com/bps-a-popular-substitute-for-bpa-in-consumer-products-may-not-be-safer-54211.

27   www.choice.com.au/food-and-drink/food-warnings-and-safety/plastic/articles/plastics-and-food.

CHAPTER 3: OLD HABITS DIE HARD

1 Freinkel, *Plastic*.
2 J. Long, N. Harré and Q.D. Atkinson, 'Understanding change in recycling and littering behavior across a school social network', *American Journal of Community Psychology*, 2014, vol. 53, no. 3–4, pp. 462–74.
3 Long, Harré and Atkinson, 'Understanding change in recycling and littering behavior across a school social network', pp. 462–74.
4 Phillippa Lally, Cornelia H.M. van Jaarsveld, Henry W.W. Potts and Jane Wardle, 'How are habits formed: Modelling habit formation in the real world', *European Journal of Social Psychology*, 2010, vol. 40, pp. 998–1009.
5 www.independent.co.uk/news/uk/home-news/queen-bans-plastic-straws-and-bottles-on-royal-estates-a8205896.html.
6 www.royal.uk/wedding-charity-donations.
7 www.townandcountrymag.com/society/tradition/a22624559/princess-eugenie-plastic-free-wedding.
8 www.abc.net.au/news/2017-05-18/abigail-forsyth-how-the-keepcup-nearly-did-not-happen/8537150.
9 www.news.com.au/finance/small-business/entrepreneurs-making-millions-from-feelgood-business-ideas/news-story/0a990d2a05c96749a942b455090c95cd.

CHAPTER 4: GETTING STARTED

1 https://wedocs.unep.org/bitstream/handle/20.500.11822/25496/singleUse-Plastic_sustainability.pdf?sequence=1&isAllowed=y, executive summary.
2 https://michaelpollan.com/reviews/just-eat-what-your-great-grandma-ate.
3 Various references, definitions such as World Commission on Environment and Development, 1987, UNEP, 1972.
4 The New Plastics Economy, Rethinking the future of plastics, World Economic Forum and Ellen MacArthur Foundation, with analytical support from McKinsey & Company, 2016, p. 15, www.ellenmacarthurfoundation.org/news/new-plastics-economy-report-offers-blueprint-to-design-a-circular-future-for-plastics.
5 Fridolin Krausmann, Simone Gingrich, Nina Eisenmenger, Karl-Heinz Erb, Helmut Haberl and Marina Fischer-Kowalski, 'Growth in global materials use,

GDP and population during the 20th century', *Journal of Ecological Economics*, 2009, vol. 68, no. 10, pp. 2696–705; 'What a Waste: A global review of solid waste management', World Bank, 2016, http://web.worldbank.org/WBSITE/EXTERNAL/TOPICS/EXTURBANDEVELOPMENT/0,,contentMDK:23172887~pagePK:210058~piPK:210062~theSitePK:337178,00.html.

6   www.environment.gov.au/system/files/resources/c8dd95af-c028-4b6e-9b23-153aecbf8c3c/files/australian-plastics-recycling-survey-report-2016-17.pdf.

7   www.nzgeo.com/stories/waste-not-want-not.

CHAPTER 5: THE KITCHEN

1   Diana Twede, 'The origins of paper-based packaging', Conference on Historical Analysis & Research in Marketing Proceedings, 2005, vol. 12, pp. 288–300.

2   www.cancentral.com/content/nicolas-appert-father-canning.

3   www.environment.gov.au/system/files/resources/d075c9bc-45b3-4ac0-a8f2-6494c7d1fa0d/files/national-waste-report-2016.pdf.

4   www.foodstandards.gov.au/consumer/chemicals/bpa/Pages/default.aspx.

5   Retail Food Sector Report 2017, Global Agricultural Information Network, https://gain.fas.usda.gov/Recent%20GAIN%20Publications/Retail%20Foods_Canberra_Australia_12-18-2017.pdf, p. 13.

6   www.smartcompany.com.au/business-advice/reusable-food-containers-gain-popularity-business-need-know.

7   www.modifiedatmospherepackaging.com/~/media/Modifiedatmospherepackaging/Brochures/MAP-Poster-Guide-2014.ashx.

8   www.modifiedatmospherepackaging.com/~/media/Modifiedatmosphere-packaging/Brochures/MAP-Poster-Guide-2014.ashx.

9   www.bbc.com/capital/story/20180705-whats-the-real-price-of-getting-rid-of-plastic-packaging.

10 www.csiro.au/en/Research/Health/Food-safety/Refrigerating-foods.

CHAPTER 6: THE LAUNDRY AND CLEANING

1   www.oversixty.com.au/lifestyle/at-home/2015/10/uses-for-sunlight-soap (also known as Velvet soap in the southern states).

2 www.slate.com/articles/health_and_science/explainer/2013/08/sunlight_is_
the_best_disinfectant_not_exactly.html.

3 www.smh.com.au/lifestyle/health-and-wellness/germ-warfare-do-
antibacterial-products-do-more-harm-than-good-20171117-gzno8i.html.

4 www.smithsonianmag.com/science-nature/five-reasons-why-you-should-
probably-stop-using-antibacterial-soap-180948078.

5 www.uq.edu.au/news/article/2018/06/toothpaste-and-hand-wash-may-
contribute-antibiotic-resistance.

6 www.oversixty.com.au/lifestyle/at-home/2015/10/uses-for-sunlight-soap.

7 www.therogueginger.com.

8 www.plasticfreejuly.org/cleaning.html.

9 www.choice.com.au/home-and-living/kitchen/dishwashers/articles/how-to-
clean-your-dishwasher.

10 Nancy Goodyear, 'Increasing delivery of healthcare at home and the import-
ance of hygiene', *Perspectives in Public Health*, 2016, vol. 136, no. 4, pp. 208–9.

11 https://davidsuzuki.org/queen-of-green/does-vinegar-kill-germs.

12 I. Falcóa, M. Verdeguerc, R. Aznara, G. Sáncheza and W. Randazzoa, 'Sanitiz-
ing food contact surfaces by the use of essential oils', *Innovative Food Science
and Emerging Technologies*, 2018, doi.org/10.1016/j.ifset.2018.02.013.

13 Anis Ben Hsouna, Nihed Ben Halima, Slim Smaoui and Naceur Hamdi, 'Citrus
lemon essential oil: Chemical composition, antioxidant and antimicrobial
activities with its preservative effect against *Listeria monocytogenes* inoculated in
minced beef meat', *Lipids in Health and Disease*, 2017, vol. 16, no.
146, doi: 10.1186/s12944-017-0487-5.

14 Jess Vergis, P. Gokulakrishnan, R.K. Agarwal and Ashok Kumar, 'Essential oils
as natural food antimicrobial agents: A review', *Critical Reviews in Food Science
and Nutrition*, 2015, vol. 55, no. 10, pp. 1320–3, doi.org/10.1080/10408398.2012
.692127.

CHAPTER 7: THE BATHROOM

1 http://query.nytimes.com/mem/archive-free/pdf?res=9904E5DA143EE233A25
753C1A9639C946997D6CF.

2 https://thenewdaily.com.au/life/wellbeing/2015/10/17/how-often-should-you-
wash-your-hair.

3   www.abs.gov.au/ausstats/abs@.nsf/Latestproducts/6530.0Main%
    20Features102015-16?opendocument&tabname=Summary&prodno=6530.0&
    issue=2015-16&num=&view=.

4   www.choice.com.au/home-and-living/household/everyday-items/review-and-
    compare/toilet-paper.

5   www.theguardian.com/environment/2016/apr/19/microplastics-which-
    beauty-brands-are-safe-to-use.

6   https://psmag.com/news/why-has-it-taken-the-menstrual-cup-so-long-to-go-
    mainstream.

7   Various references including *Choice*, www.choice.com.au/health-and-body/
    reproductive-health/womens-health/articles/menstrual-cups-and-period-
    underwear#what%20haven't%20I%20heard%20of%20them%202.

8   www.theguardian.com/environment/2017/oct/29/the-eco-guide-to-
    period-dramas.

9   https://lifewithoutplastic.com/store/blog/plastic-free-periods-using-reusable-
    alternatives.

CHAPTER 8: YOUR WARDROBE

1   Fashion at the Crossroads, Greenpeace, 2017 https://storage.googleapis.com/
    p4-production-content/international/wp-content/uploads/2017/09/76e05528-
    fashion-at-the-crossroads.pdf.

2   Fashion at the Crossroads, Greenpeace.

3   Read more at www.business2community.com/fashion-beauty/30-shocking-
    figures-facts-global-textile-apparel-industry-01222057.

4   Kosuke Tanaka and Hideshige Takada, 'Microplastic fragments and
    microbeads in digestive tracts of planktivorous fish from urban coastal
    waters', *Scientific Reports*, 2016, vol. 6, no. 34351.

5   Kate Finnigan, 'Plastic is not cool'—Is fashion finally cleaning up its act?', *The
    Guardian*, 8 June 2018 www.theguardian.com/fashion/2018/jun/07/plastic-is-
    not-cool-is-fashion-finally-cleaning-up-its-act.

6   Editorial, *Sportwear International*, Spring 2018, p. 3.

7   http://rozaliaproject.org/stop-microfiber-pollution.

8   www.abc.net.au/news/2017-05-21/scientists-warn-of-growing-cost-of-inac-
    tion-on-microfibres/8540606.

9   https://fashionunited.uk/news/fashion/sustainable-textile-innovations-coffee-ground-fibre/2017061624856.

10 https://theconversation.com/sustainable-shopping-for-eco-friendly-jeans-stop-washing-them-so-often-75781.

11 http://wedocs.unep.org/bitstream/handle/20.500.11822/25485/plastic_altern-ative.pdf?sequence=1&isAllowed=y.

12 www.qmilkfiber.eu/qmilk-faser-modische-anwendung?lang=en.

13 www.businessinsider.com.au/how-tencel-compares-to-cotton-2015-9?r=US&IR=T.

CHAPTER 9: PLASTIC-FREE KIDS

1   www.independent.co.uk/environment/plastic-pollution-waste-uk-families-shopping-environment-recycling-use-supermarket-a8223711.html.

2   www.sustainability.vic.gov.au/You-and-Your-Home/Live-sustainably/Single-use-items/Balloons.

3   www.choice.com.au/food-and-drink/food-warnings-and-safety/plastic/articles/plastics-and-food.

4   www.sustainability.vic.gov.au/You-and-Your-Home/Live-sustainably/Single-use-items/Nappies.

5   www.choice.com.au/babies-and-kids/baby-clothes-and-nappies/nappies/buying-guides/disposable-and-cloth-nappies.

6   www.thetimes.co.uk/article/billions-of-food-pouches-go-to-landfill-c7hf6lwc6.

7   https://qz.com/1340729/the-wild-success-of-baby-food-pouches-shows-how-weve-embraced-the-idea-of-food-as-utility.

8   www.wired.com/story/lego-sustainable-bricks.

9   www.sciencedirect.com/science/article/pii/S0163638317301613.

CHAPTER 10: ENTERTAINING, AND EATING (AND DRINKING) OUT

1   www.abc.net.au/news/health/2017-05-17/is-it-safe-to-eat-food-after-cut-mould-off/8518220.

2   www.therobincollective.co.uk/kfc-edible-cups.

3   https://wedocs.unep.org/bitstream/handle/20.500.11822/25485/plastic_altern-ative.pdf?sequence=1&isAllowed=y, p. 66.

CHAPTER 11: THE END OF SINGLE-USE PLASTIC?

1   www.theguardian.com/environment/2018/may/16/new-labelling-helps-uk-shoppers-avoid-plastic-packaging.

2   www.european-bioplastics.org/electrolux-builds-the-worlds-first-bioplastic-concept-fridge.

3   https://crawfordpackaging.com/produce-packaging-101/top-trends.

4   www.packagingcovenant.org.au/news/empowering-australian-businesses-to-meet-their-sustainable-packaging-obligations.

5   www.unilever.com/news/press-releases/2017/Unilever-commits-to-100-percent-recyclable-plastic.html.

6   www.plasticsnewseurope.com/assets/PDF/PN11458539.PDF.

7   www.progressbiomaterials.com/content/2/1/8.

8   The New Plastics Economy', https://newplasticseconomy.org.

9   https://storyofstuff.org/blog/the-plastic-straw-starbucks-and-a-movement-at-a-crossroads.